D1391142

The History of the
MIDDLE EAST WARS

The History of the
MIDDLE EAST WARS

J. N. Westwood

Bison Books

Published by
Bison Books Ltd.
176 Old Brompton Road,
London SW 5
England.

Copyright © 1984 Bison Books Ltd.

All rights reserved. No part of this publication
may be reproduced, stored in a retrieval system
or transmitted in any form by any means electronic,
mechanical, photocopying or otherwise, without
first obtaining written permission of the
copyright owner.

ISBN 0 86124 166 5

Printed in Hong Kong

Reprinted 1988

PAGE 1: *Members of the
IDF enter a terrorist
hideout in Beirut.*
PAGE 2–3: *Armored cars of
the Arab Legion in the
West Bank in 1949.*
PAGE 4–5: *Right-wing
Christian militiamen
reload an artillery piece in
the Chouf Mountains, 1983.*

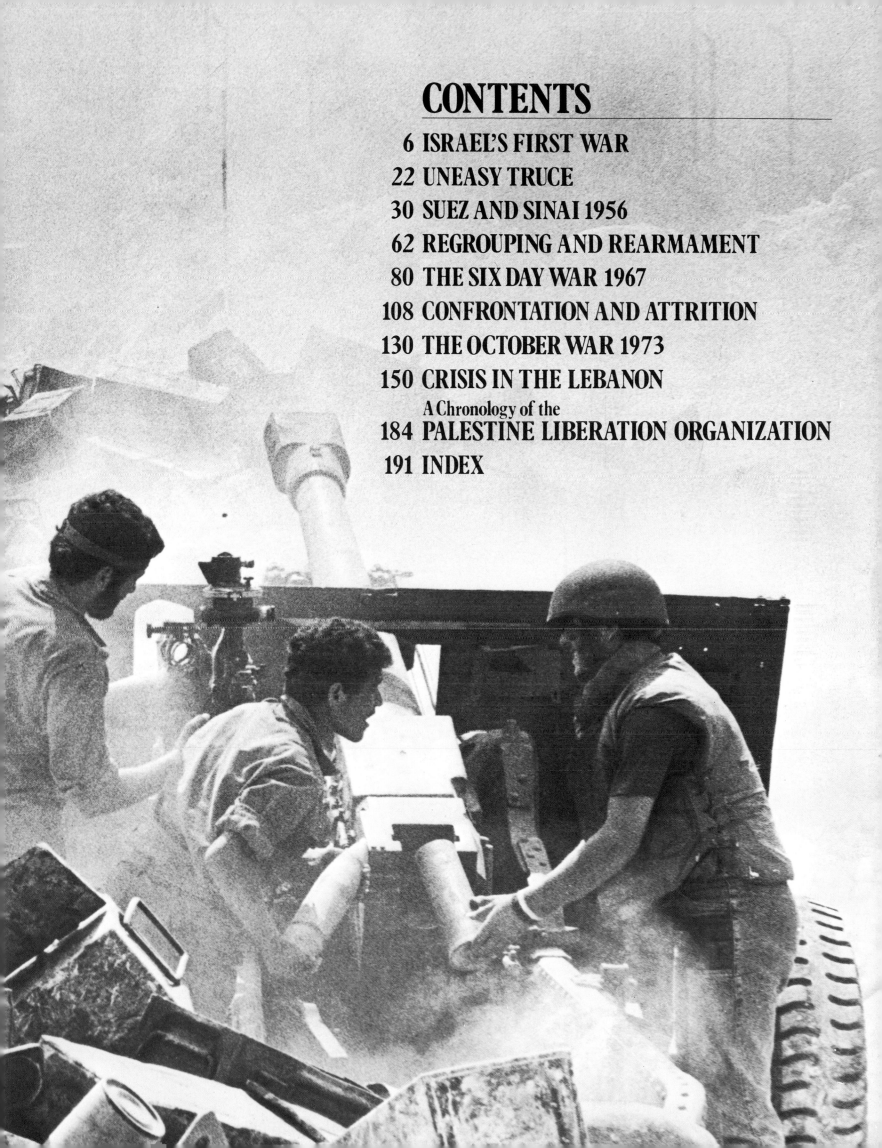

CONTENTS

ISRAEL'S FIRST WAR

Already longer than the Thirty Years' War, shorter as yet than the Hundred Years' War, the Middle East War of the mid- and late 20th century shares at least one common factor with these, in that it consists of a series of full-scale conflicts, interspersed with periods of recovery, rearmament, diplomacy and argument. When wars continue for decades the generations which endure them may ask what it is all about, and wonder whether their leaders could not have found a better way to settle their differences.

During its course outside parties have intervened on such a scale that the original conflict which underlies the Middle East War has sometimes been obscured. Despite the earlier involvement of France and Britain, this is not and was not an imperialist war. Despite the involvement of the USSR and the USA, this war is not primarily a struggle between the superpowers. Despite the circumstance that the forces of several Arab states have been ranged against Israel, this is not a war about Arab unity. It is a war which was started simply to decide whether Jews or Arabs should have their own domain in Palestine, and this is the first issue which must be settled before the state of violence can come to an end.

In 1897 the Zionist Organization was founded in Vienna, with the aim of re-establishing a Jewish homeland in Palestine. At first it achieved little, although the British government was sufficiently aware of the Jewish problem to offer some territory in the Sinai Desert for this purpose, an offer that was rejected by the Zionists, who wanted something better. Meanwhile, using the Jewish population already in Palestine as a foundation, the Zionists established scattered and usually isolated agricultural communities in that area, which was still part of the Ottoman Empire.

Britain's unhappy involvement with the Palestine problem began in 1917. Fighting, and far from winning, a desperate war against Germany, Austria, and Turkey, the government was willing to take long-term risks for short-term gains. Needing American support, and especially financial support, and realizing the influence wielded by American Jews, Britain took the fateful step of declaring its official support for a Palestinian Jewish homeland. This took the form of the Balfour Declaration, which contained a provision that the British hoped would provide an escape should the commitment prove impracticable; this provision stipulated that any settlement of Jewish immigrants should not prejudice the rights of the Palestinian Arabs. The Balfour Declaration could therefore be interpreted by the Jews as a promise of a homeland, and by the Arabs as a promise that their own homeland (the same territory) would not be disturbed by the Jewish immigrants. Possibly, if Britain

ABOVE: *Orde Wingate, who instructed the* Haganah.
PREVIOUS PAGES: *Bofors gunners of the Arab Legion in 1949.*

had kept out of Middle Eastern affairs, this Declaration would have remained innocuous, but as things turned out, Britain became responsible for the government of Palestine in the interwar period. This development also had its beginnings in 1917, when General Allenby marched his victorious Anglo-Indian army into Jerusalem, ending the centuries-old administration by Turkey. Soon after the war, the League of Nations granted a mandate (a temporary right of administration) for Britain to take charge of Palestine.

In 1917, about 85,000 Jews lived in Palestine, these being mainly families that had remained in the area since ancient times. Sincerely adhering to the Balfour Declaration, the British allowed Jewish immigrants to increase so that by 1947 the Jewish population was about 600,000, compared with an Arab population of over 1,000,000. This influx generated first distrust, and then fear, on the part of the Palestinian Arabs, and their anxieties were exploited by the local Muslem priesthood. The Palestinian Arabs, just like the Palestinian Jews, lived in a culture in which the established church was also the main political influence. The Muslim Mufti of Jerusalem, Haj Amin el Husseini, was quick to incite his Arab flock to

rebellion, starting with disturbances in 1922 and 1929, and ending with a more serious revolt in 1936. The Mufti had been arrested by the British soon after they took over, but had been released as a goodwill gesture; it took several decades for the British to understand that in the Middle East goodwill gestures rarely produce goodwill. Husseini was finally expelled after the 1936 revolt, and until his death in 1974 played a progressively declining role as inciter-in-exile.

In their hopeless attempt to meet the wishes of both Jews and Arabs, the British had sought to ensure that most of Palestine would be reserved for the latter. Winston Churchill, who in 1922 was Colonial Secretary, created an autonomous (though not independent) Transjordan that occupied the part of Palestine on the eastern side of the River Jordan, as well as a considerable part on the west bank. Soon to become a kingdom under King Abdullah, Transjordan occupied four-fifths of Palestine. After the Arab revolt of 1936 the British began to realize the scale of the problem they faced, and a Royal Commission of Enquiry set to work in 1937. Its bleak conclusion was that Jews and Arabs would never come to a compromise enabling them to live tranquilly side by side. Hence the only viable solution was to partition Palestine: this should be Transjordan for the Arabs, a new Jewish state for the Jews, while Jerusalem (a holy city not only for Muslims and Jews but for Christians as well) would remain under British mandate and therefore be accessible to visitors of all religions. The Arab community, partly by natural inclination but largely under the influence of its priestly leaders, rejected this solution. Failing Arab agreement, the British were disinclined to impose this solution by force and, until World War II changed the picture, British policy continued to be one of muddling-through, even though it was realized that muddle-through only worked when opposing passions could be expected to cool as time passed. Thanks partly to religious incitement, partly to the very intractability of the problem, years in which violence declined were occupied not by a cooling of passions but by a fanning of embers. This is a pattern which has continued to the present day.

The Arab revolt of 1936 marks the beginning of a turbulent period that has continued into the 1980s. The revolt was directed against Jews, and the latter, to protect themselves against roving bands of armed Arabs, organized their own local home guards, the *Haganah* (more formally, *Irgun Hahaganah* or 'Organization for Defense). The *Haganah*'s policy was strictly one of self-defense, but for some Jews of more violent temperament that was not enough, and they founded the *Irgun Zvai Leumi*, or IZL. This, which came to be led by Menachem Begin, was originally an underground movement specializing in retaliatory actions against Arabs, but rapidly deteriorated into a drab terrorist organization whose effect was to make a bad situation worse, presumably in the expectation that violent chaos would produce a situation in which it would flourish. That Menachem Begin would subsequently receive the Nobel Peace Prize is one of the more piquant reminders that in the Arab-Israeli conflict the transition from the incredible to the plausible may be swift.

The IZL tended to be anti-British as well as anti-Arab, whereas the *Haganah* was simply pro-Jewish. But even the IZL stopped its attacks on Britons in 1939, for Hitler's Germany was too obvious a menace to allow any other decision. But in 1944, when Hitler seemed beaten, the IZL again began to murder British personnel in Palestine. The *Haganah*, however, continued to co-operate with the British administration. This co-operation dated from before the war when, among other things, the *Haganah* was taught by the British army officer Orde Wingate, of subsequent Chindit fame; Wingate's job was to instruct the *Haganah* in night operations designed to protect the Iraq-Haifa oil pipeline, a favorite target of Arab bands. In 1944 a Jewish brigade group was fighting on the Allied side in Italy. Earlier, the future Israeli Defense Minister Moshe Dayan lost an eye when fighting for the British; his *Haganah* unit was supporting British troops against the

Vichy French in Syria. In this latter campaign, but in a different battlefield, the British-officered Arab Legion of Transjordan also fought on the British side.

It was only in 1945 that the complete story of the near-extermination of Jews in Nazi-occupied Europe became known, although there had long been an awareness of Jewish persecution. Having done nothing specific to help the Jews survive during the war, some of the victorious countries, and especially the newly liberated states of Europe whose own consciences were not entirely carefree in the matter of anti-Semitism, began to see in the creation of a Palestinian homeland a cause in support of which they might not

only acquire virtue at no cost to themselves, but also solve their own problem of what to do with the mass of Jewish 'displaced persons' for whom homes had to be found. An early manifestation of this movement in opinion was President Truman's request that the British allow 100,000 homeless Jews to settle in Palestine. The British, on the eve of the war, had imposed limits on Jewish immigration into Palestine, at a time when thousands of Jewish refugees were arriving from Hitler's Germany. This had attracted much bitter criticism, and their 1945 refusal to accept the US president's request added to their unpopularity. International Jewish organizations began to send shiploads of

ABOVE: *Illegal immigrants reach Haifa, 1946.*
LEFT: *The minesweeper HMS* Rowena *intercepts a ship carrying illegal Jewish immigrants and plays a fire hose on the more hostile elements.*

illegal immigrants to Palestine; whenever these ships were intercepted and turned back by the Royal Navy, fresh condemnation was heaped upon the hapless British. Inside Palestine, the *Haganah* now led the armed opposition, concentrating at first on bringing in the illegal immigrants. The IZL, despite its predilection for bloodshed, was found to be too tame by many Jews, who joined the more aggressive Stern Gang.

The *Haganah*, despite arrests of its more prominent commanders, began a successful campaign of destroying bridges on roads leading into the neighboring Arab states. War-weary Britain found itself obliged to maintain an army of about 10,000 men in Palestine merely to prevent disaster, and with no end in sight. Pressure, especially from the US government and inside the new United Nations Organization, was directed toward persuading London to adopt a more pro-Jewish attitude (or, in the opinion of critics, a less anti-Jewish attitude). The British government, for strategic reasons anxious to

LEFT: *Casualties are carried from the rubble of the King David Hotel, July 1946.*
RIGHT: *The Arab Legion, Jerusalem, 1949.*

retain what was left of Arab goodwill throughout the Middle East, resisted these pressures until February 1947, when Foreign Secretary Ernest Bevin announced that Britain would place the problem in the hands of the United Nations.

There then followed the final, and unhappiest, year of the British mandate. The IZL blew up the British HQ in Jerusalem, the King David Hotel, killing scores of soldiers. The British executed members of the IZL and Stern Gang, and the latter retaliated by kidnapping and hanging British soldiers. In the outside world, the British interception of the illegal immigrant ship *Exodus*, and the return of its passengers to Germany, brought anti-British outcry to a new and skillfully orchestrated level. Inside Palestine, British officers tried to be even-handed, despite a growing animosity toward the Jews, but this policy pleased nobody and seemed inconsistent. In May 1948 the last British troops left the country.

The British withdrawal was certainly inglorious, and throughout the British mandate policy had been muddled both in concept and execution, while successive British governments had been reluctant, as are all democratic governments, to grasp nettles. To this extent criticism of British conduct is justified. But accusations of hypocrisy and scheming seem wide of the mark. Britain's misfortune was that it had chosen to be in the wrong place at the wrong time, a place and time when

the characteristic British solutions of patience and compromise (sometimes describable as inaction) had no chance of success. In many ways, the quarter-century that followed the British mandate was no improvement on the quarter-century that preceded the withdrawal.

The UN was no more able to solve the problem than Britain had been, although it had the advantage of worldwide support for its resolutions. It appointed a special commission which visited Palestine and in the course of a few weeks discovered what the British knew already. Not surprisingly, its recommendations seemed to repeat the conclusions of the British 1937 Royal Commission; it suggested that Palestine be split into Arab and Jewish states, with the city of Jerusalem entrusted to international trusteeship. The UN General Assembly voted overwhelmingly for this scheme in November 1947, with the USA and USSR voting in favor, and Britain abstaining. The Arab states not only voted against this partition plan but began to try to prevent its implementation.

The UN commission had experienced considerable difficulty in deciding the frontiers of the new Jewish state. Although in Palestine there were areas and towns that were predominantly Jewish or Arab, the two peoples lived side by side and it was impossible to declare a given area to be Jewish or Arab without upsetting the minority population. As a result of careful investigation, it was possible, but only just,

to delineate a continuous territory as the proposed Jewish state, but this territory contained numerous Arab settlements, while many Jewish localities remained outside its frontiers. Even so, the new state was inevitably misshapen. It ran from north to south for less than 400 miles, but only in its southern half did it broaden out into more than a narrow strip, and even here it was nowhere more than 90 miles wide. It consisted of a northern part, Galilee, bordering Syria and the Lebanon, a central coastal strip including such large towns as Haifa, Tel Aviv, and Jaffa, and the broad south, the Negev. Where these parts joined, access was constricted, with only a narrow corridor providing a link. The proposed Arab state was equally misshapen, divided into three parts and with correspondingly constricted access between these parts. Deep in the proposed Arab state lay Jerusalem, where 100,000 Jews lived; these were mainly in the New City, but some lived in the largely Arab Old City.

Since the Arab population's leaders had totally rejected partition, and were assured of support from nearby Arab states, and since partition was the only solution that had been internationally accepted as the replacement of the British mandate, it was clear that as soon as the British departed there would be a violent struggle between the Jews and Arabs, each fighting bitterly for what they regarded as their territorial rights. The months before the final British withdrawal, scheduled for May 1948, were therefore spent by both sides in strengthening their armed forces and winning tactical advantage. On a local scale hostilities were already in full swing in early 1948 as each side tried to hold or conquer strategically placed settlements. At the same time, attempts were made to purloin weapons from British depots; in this the Jews were most successful, although neither side made spectacular acquisitions in this way.

To its ultimate downfall, the local Arab population placed great confidence in the armies of the neighboring Arab states, and was less energetic than the Jews in establishing its own armed forces. By tradition, local sheikhs could summon all men of a district for a particular operation; most Arabs carried arms as a matter of course. However, this was a rather archaic practice, valuable only in strictly localized conflicts. There were indeed two organizations (the *Najada* and *Futuwa*) which could be described as paramilitary; they were useful mainly for reconnaissance and as links between the local sheikhs' men. When Jewish terrorist organizations appeared, these Arab groups turned their attention to urban guerrilla styles of opera-

tion also, but were never highly sophisticated performers in this field. The only true all-Palestine Arab forces were the two guerrilla organizations answering to the exiled Mufti jointly known as the Army of Salvation, and amounting to some 2000 men. One was led by the Mufti's cousin, Abd el Kader el-Husseimi, and the other by Hassan Salameh, who had been trained, obviously inadequately, by the Germans during the war. The independent guerrilla force in the south, organized by Egypt's Muslim Brotherhood, was too chaotic to be regarded as militarily significant except in situations where the balance of forces was very critical.

Of the Arab armies poised to enter Palestine as soon as the British left, the Arab Legion was the best trained. Glubb Pasha, who commanded it, was a British officer of World War I experience and had collected a group of Arabic-speaking British officers to assist him. Its men were Bedouin tribesmen and the combination of British discipline and Bedouin tradition was formidable. It had about 10,000 men, and included some armor and artillery. King Abdullah of Transjordan drew most of his strength and much of his influence from his possession of this first-class fighting force. The army of King Farouk of Egypt was rather larger, being the biggest of the Arab armies, but Farouk was willing to send only a 5000-strong force into Palestine. The Iraqi Army, though smaller than the Egyptian, allocated 10,000 men to the operation, and they included an armored battalion; later a Saudi Arabian contingent operated with the Iraqis. All these expeditionary forces were influenced in their organization and training by British practice, but two other Arab armies of intervention, the Syrian and Lebanese, had a French background. The Syrians allotted a force of 8000 men, which included a mechanized battalion equipped with French-built tanks, while the Lebanese fielded a 2000-man force. The Syrians also contributed a small air force.

The Arab forces which were to invade Palestine were small by World War II standards, comprising about 30,000 men with rather limited armor, artillery and air support. But they were to attack from several directions against Jewish forces that were tiny, and not so much ill-equipped as nonequipped. One of the two weaknesses of the Arabs was the difficulty of co-ordinating the separate armies, due partly to geography but much more to the rivalries and suspicion which soured the relationships between nominally fraternal regimes. The second was the circumstance that the invading soldiers were not fighting for their own homelands; despite all the propaganda to which they were subjected and in which they believed, they were less prepared for self-sacrifice than were the Jews. They were fighting somebody else's war whereas the Jews were fighting their

own battle and really did believe that death was no worse than defeat.

There were several causes of suspicion between the Arab leaders, but dominant was the distrust they felt toward King Abdullah of Transjordan. Abdullah not only possessed what was believed to be the most effective army in the Middle East, but also seemed likely to be the main beneficiary of the expected victory. Transjordan effectively was already part of Palestine and was well placed to absorb the territorial gains expected to be made at the expense of the Jews. It was largely to put a check on Abdullah that the Arab leadership created its own jointly owned Arab Liberation Army, or ALA. Nominally headed by an Iraqi, this volunteer force was led by a charismatic Syrian, Fauzi el Kaukji, who had once been an officer in the Ottoman Army and had led Arab irregular forces in the 1936 revolt with a certain dash, accompanied by more than a certain lack of success.

ABOVE: *David Ben-Gurion became the first Prime Minister of Israel in May 1948.*

ABOVE: *Volunteers of the Jordanian National Guard being trained, 1949.*
RIGHT: *An Israeli mortar crew, 1948.*

Some months before the UN resolution in favor of partition, the Jewish authorities in Palestine had begun to make preparations for war. These authorities were essentially the Jewish Agency, which under the British mandate had been set up to allow Palestinian Jews to regulate their own affairs. Headed by David Ben-Gurion, it was a limited form of self-government. Among other things, the British had allowed it to finance a 2000-man armed police force, the Jewish Settlement Police which, however, had British officers. By 1947 Ben-Gurion had a much-strengthened *Haganah* at his disposal. This loose self-defense organization had been overhauled when World War II spread to the Middle East, and within it had been created full-time units collectively known as the *Palmach*. The latter, despite deficiencies

of weapons and of training, was regarded as an elite by the Jewish population, and indeed the *Palmach* of the early 1940s is interesting because so many of its young officers later became Israeli generals and ministers. The *Palmach*, and the armed forces in general, were much strengthened in 1947 and 1948 when there was an influx of veterans of World War II, former members of the Jewish Brigade Group and Jewish members of wartime Allied armies. The arrival of these men, volunteers in the fight for existence of the new Jewish state, brought much-needed experience and technical skill.

In 1947 the *Palmach* had about 3000 soldiers of both sexes. In addition, the Jewish population could produce about 12,000 full-time recruits in case of need, with a further 30,000 men and women part-timers for the defense of their own settlements. But less than a thousand rifles, and perhaps a similar number of machine guns, were available, and even for these there was ammunition for only a few days of fighting. Unlike the opposing Arab armies poised on the frontiers, the Jewish forces had no armored units, although some home-made armored cars existed, typically trucks fitted with metal plates and machine guns. In the air, too, the *Haganah*'s air platoon seemed pathetically outnumbered by its expected opponents. It possessed a mere 11 civilian light aircraft, single or twin seaters, with 20 pilots to fly them, together with about 20 former fighter pilots of the Royal Air Force who, however, had no fighters to fly.

BELOW: *A member of the* Irgun Zvai Leumi *mounts guard.*

In the early weeks of the hostilities the IZL and Stern Gang also made useful contributions, the former having 2000–3000 members, and the Stern Gang about 1000. But their extreme and sometimes brutal conduct, their inability to engage in operations where discipline was required, and their frequent refusal to co-ordinate their operations with those of the *Haganah*, meant that they soon became more of an embarrassment than an asset.

British Army deserters played a role which may have been important, but their activities were, understandably, little publicized by the British or by the Arabs and Jews. Probably one of the reasons for the British withdrawal from responsibility in Palestine was the desertion rate of the large army stationed there. Soldiers who had endured the years of World War II in the knowledge that they were suffering for a noble cause were less steadfast when they found themselves miles from home, trying to keep the peace between two peoples while being shot at by both. To these 'natural' deserters were added British soldiers of Jewish origin (and a few of Arab background) who wanted to take an active part. Israel's first tanks were a pair of British Army Cromwell units brought over by deserters. The Arabs succeeded in two terrorist attacks in Jerusalem, exploding heavy charges and killing scores of passers-by, by using British Army deserters in uniform, driving stolen British Army trucks loaded with explosives.

The British mandate expired at midnight on 14 May 1948. In a move which anticipated a Jewish solution to many difficult circumstances, Ben-Gurion announced the new state of Israel at midday,

12 hours prematurely (perhaps to avoid the Sabbath), and this was followed within an hour or so by US recognition of the new state, evidence enough in Arab eyes of the close collusion between Palestinian Jews and the American government. Soviet recognition came three days later, but the British and French held back until early 1949. As it was obvious that the Arab coalition was resolved to send in its troops at the moment when the last British flag was lowered, Ben-Gurion's move was understandable. With so much to do and to organize, a 12-hour lead was invaluable.

The resulting war of 1948–49 was scattered both in time and place. In time, its divisions were marked by truces, and in location by the different but theoretically convergent directions of the Arab advance. The Israeli command faced a war on several fronts, including an internal front, and its role was to direct the movements of its small forces on a day-to-day basis, allocating priorities according to what appeared to be the immediate crisis of the time. It did have the advantage of being a single seat of control, whereas the Arab armies were only nominally under co-ordinated leadership. The Israelis also had the advantage of internal lines of communication, enabling them to dispatch troops from one front to another. But this advantage was reduced by scattered Arab forces that occupied high ground dominating key roads inside Israel. Although the permutations of time and place make it difficult to describe this campaign coherently one circumstance is clear, although sometimes overlooked: this was essentially a small-scale and primitive war between small units. The Israeli 'front'

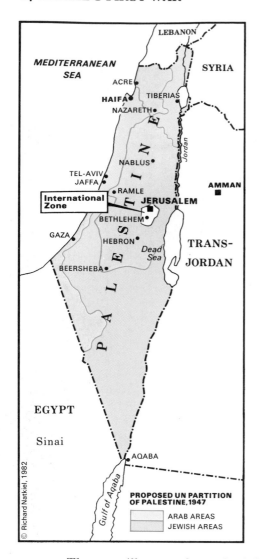

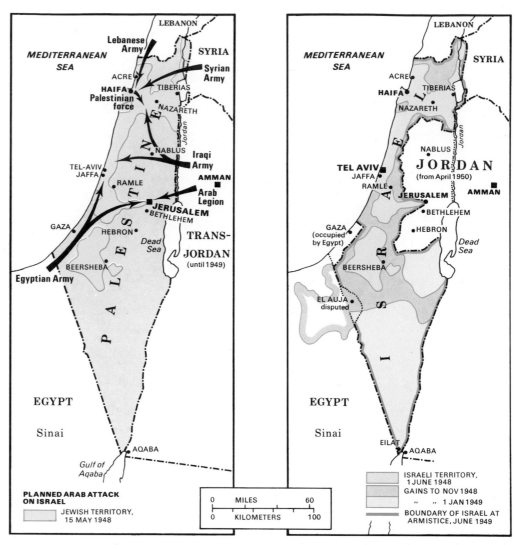

MEDITERRANEAN SEA
LEBANON
SYRIA
ACRE
HAIFA
TIBERIAS
NAZARETH
TEL-AVIV
JAFFA
NABLUS
RAMLE
International Zone
JERUSALEM
BETHLEHEM
GAZA
HEBRON
Dead Sea
BEERSHEBA
TRANS-JORDAN
AMMAN
EGYPT
Sinai
AQABA
Gulf of Aqaba

© Richard Natkiel, 1982

PROPOSED UN PARTITION OF PALESTINE, 1947
ARAB AREAS
JEWISH AREAS

MEDITERRANEAN SEA
LEBANON
Lebanese Army
SYRIA
Syrian Army
ACRE
HAIFA
Palestinian force
TIBERIAS
NAZARETH
TEL-AVIV
JAFFA
NABLUS
Iraqi Army
RAMLE
AMMAN
Arab Legion
GAZA
JERUSALEM
BETHLEHEM
HEBRON
Dead Sea
BEERSHEBA
TRANS-JORDAN
(until 1949)
Egyptian Army
EGYPT
Sinai
AQABA
Gulf of Aqaba

PLANNED ARAB ATTACK ON ISRAEL
JEWISH TERRITORY, 15 MAY 1948

0 MILES 60
0 KILOMETERS 100

MEDITERRANEAN SEA
LEBANON
SYRIA
ACRE
HAIFA
TIBERIAS
NAZARETH
NABLUS
JORDAN (from April 1950)
TEL AVIV
JAFFA
RAMLE
JERUSALEM
AMMAN
GAZA (occupied by Egypt)
BETHLEHEM
HEBRON
Dead Sea
BEERSHEBA
EL AUJA disputed
EGYPT
Sinai
EILAT
AQABA

ISRAELI TERRITORY, 1 JUNE 1948
GAINS TO NOV 1948
" " 1 JAN 1949
BOUNDARY OF ISRAEL AT ARMISTICE, JUNE 1949

ABOVE: *The maps illustrate the territorial gains of the state of Israel up to June 1949.*

was simply a collection of brigades, and brigades were basic formations; divisions, corps, and armies belonged to World War II, not to this war. The disposition of the main Israeli strength, its *Palmach* brigades, ensured that each brigade covered a likely Arab advance, with brigades additionally allocated to Tel Aviv and Jerusalem, the two main Jewish population centers.

The war may be divided into six periods. The period of civil war in fact began with skirmishes before the British left and continued to 15 May 1948, when the Arab forces invaded, introducing the second period which lasted until the truce of 11 June. This truce came to a violent end on 9 July, with the 'Nine Day War' lasting until a new truce of 18 July. This latter truce endured uneasily until 15 October, when the final period began. This ended in 1949, with the belligerent Arab governments, typically enough, signing individual armistices with Israel on different dates, Egypt being the first (in January) and Syria the last (in July). Israeli historians have claimed that because of anti-Israel majorities in the United Nations, the latter imposed truces whenever the Israeli forces were poised for victory. There is possibly

an element of truth in this, insofar as the UN seemed less decisive at times when Israel seemed at its last gasp. On the other hand, since time was more vital to Israel than to the Arabs (time to acquire arms abroad, time to organize the Israel Defense Forces) the truces were probably more beneficial to Israel than to its enemies.

In the civil-war phase, strangulation of Israeli communications was the Arab strategy. Although there were large Jewish concentrations in the cities, most of the Jewish population was in scattered agricultural settlements. Although these organized their own defense, they relied for supply and reinforcement on the few highways. The latter often passed through Arab settlements, or at least were dominated by high ground which could be occupied by local Arab forces. Jewish operations, usually with a *Palmach* brigade as a nucleus, therefore tended to be directed toward the capture of this high ground. Operation *Jephtha*, which lasted 10 days in April, was one of the more important battles of this type. Its aim, to clear the highway between Tiberias and Rosh Pina, entailed the capture of Safed, a town of 12,000 inhabitants, of whom 10,000 were Arabs. The Arab civilians fled on the approach of the Jewish forces, leaving a 2000-man garrison of ALA and armed locals which conducted a desperate but unsuccessful defense.

ABOVE: *King Abdullah of Transjordan.*
RIGHT: *West Bank woman cleans a Bren.*

Already the *Haganah* was reorganizing itself and its objectives. Soon to reach a strength of 40,000, its aim was to occupy, as the British withdrew, not only the territory allocated to the Jews under the partition plan but also areas within terri-

tory allocated to the Arabs which were predominantly Jewish or were considered essential for the defense of the new Jewish state in the event of an Arab invasion. The British withdrew progressively, area by area, and the Jewish and Arab forces competed to fill the resulting gaps. The case of Safed was not untypical. Here the outnumbered Jewish population, concentrated in the lower town, had been virtually under Arab siege since February, despite the British presence; the location of the Arabs in the dominant upper town made this almost inevitable. The British were scheduled to withdraw from this town on 15 April, but before this a *Palmach* platoon had infiltrated into the lower town. As the British vacated their strongpoints in the upper town the Arabs were able to occupy them within minutes. Yigal Allon, commander of the *Palmach*, realized that Arab-held Safed could dominate northern Galilee, and that is why it was decided to capture it even at the risk of heavy losses.

More important than the seizure of Safed was the securing of Haifa, an important port whose population of 200,000 was equally divided between Arabs and Jews. In late April the British began the first phase of their withdrawal here, evacuating several strongpoints and concentrating in a few military camps. Operation Scissors of the *Palmach* Carmeli Brigade was undertaken to cope with this situation. The Brigade swept into the city from the nearby Carmel high ground, taking the Arabs by surprise and splitting the Arab part of the city into three isolated sections. The local Arab commander thereupon fled to nearby Lebanon and the British commander, Major General Stockwell, in accordance with general British policy, tried to calm the situation without involving British forces in any fighting. He called a meeting of Jewish and Arab elders, at which the Jews demanded that the Arabs should hand over their arms, while asking them to continue living in Haifa. At the urging of representatives of the exiled Mufti and of the ALA commander, el Kaukji, the Arab leaders decided to evacuate their citizens, all but a few thousand of whom took to the road as refugees. In this way Haifa became a Jewish city.

No doubt the Arabs of Haifa were influenced by the anticipation that within a few weeks the invading Arab armies would restore them to their homes and offer them the opportunity of profiting from an elimination of the Jewish inhabitants. As things turned out, they and their children and unborn grandchildren were destined to remain homeless refugees. It should be added that warnings of massacres by triumphant Jews, should the Arabs have remained in the city, were not entirely baseless. The exodus of Arabs from Jewish Palestine in 1948 and the

creation of the long-standing and fateful Palestinian refugee problem was not simply the product of ill-based, perhaps ill-intentioned, advice offered by the Mufti and his priestly representatives. Such an exodus was of obvious advantage to the new state of Israel, which benefited from the departure of a potentially hostile section of the population and at the same time became a more homogeneous Jewish state. The leaders of Israel, who were neither callous nor short-sighted opportunists, were almost certainly sincere in their declared wish to retain the Arab population. On the other hand, to some influential Jews it seemed obvious that Jewish rights to their allocated territory would be immeasurably stronger and more valuable if the Arabs left. This section of opinion, it seems, was sufficiently widespread to ensure that in the battles of 1948 it was not unknown for victorious Israeli forces to chase out, with bullet and mortar bomb, the Arab populations of captured settlements. Furthermore, although news of scattered Jewish atrocities was rapidly exaggerated into grotesque rumors, there is no doubt that massacres of Arab populations did occur, as did killings of Jewish populations by Arabs. Such massacres, like the large-scale killings at Deir Yassin in April, may have been the work of the IZL or Stern Gang, and were clearly at variance with the Jewish leaders' intentions, but for those Arabs in the path of an Israeli advance this was a fine distinction.

The Deir Yassin massacre was an unfortunate and quite unnecessary event in the battles which comprised Operation *Nachschon*, an ultimately successful campaign to clear the highway from Tel Aviv to Jerusalem. Jerusalem, deep inside terri-

TOP: *Jewish defenders of Safed.*
ABOVE: *Yigal Allon, commander of the* Palmach, *at the wheel of his jeep in 1948.*

tory allotted to the Arabs, had a large Jewish population that, like so many other outlying Jewish settlements, was supplied by armed truck convoys. Here, as elsewhere, Arab attacks on convoys were proving so costly that an attempt had to be made to secure the high ground that commanded much of the route. At the western end of the road about 1500 men captured Hulda and Deir Muheisin from the Arabs in early April, but were soon ordered to quit by the British. Closer to Jerusalem, Kastel was captured by the Jews. These successes allowed a convoy of 60 trucks to reach Jerusalem. The Arabs, with ALA units in the lead, then counter-attacked and Kastel, among others, changed hands several times. After a week the Jewish forces holding Kastel were reduced to one man, whose eventual retreat coincided with the death of the Arab commander, Kader el-Husseini. The latter had strolled into another Jewish position, believing it to be Arab-held. Demoralized by the loss of their leader, the Arabs withdrew and Kastel was finally reoccupied by fresh Jewish forces. For a few precious days convoys took supplies to Jerusalem, enabling the Jewish forces there to hold out for another two valuable months. Although the Arabs managed to close the route again, their defeat here, together with Kaukji's earlier failure to capture the strategic Jewish settlement of Mishmar Haemek, between Tel Aviv and Haifa, was a psychological boost to the Jews and a psychological reverse for the Arabs, while Kaukji's failure additionally discredited and unnerved the ALA.

It was during the struggle for Kastel that IZL and Stern Gang units, with *Haganah* support, captured the nearby Arab village of Deir Yassin. After the capture the *Haganah* departed to fight elsewhere, leaving the IZL and Stern Gang in occupation. Over 250 men, women and children, the surviving population, were then killed. The Jewish Agency not only

ABOVE: *Jewish villagers at Montefiore, near Jerusalem, come under sniper fire.*
LEFT: *Friendly Arabs at Safed in Galilee.*

denied any prior knowledge of this atrocity but even sent a message of condolence to King Abdullah of Transjordan. Here and there, in these weeks, Jews were massacred by Arabs. In early May in fighting around Jerusalem an Arab Legion company, theoretically attached to the British Army, captured the Jewish Etzion settlements, and was followed by Arab villagers who shot the Jewish prisoners.

Until the Etzion misfortune, Jewish policy had been to defend all Jewish settlements, whatever the cost. But with the war intensifying, this was a policy which did not pay, especially as Arab regular soldiers were now among the attackers. In the following months purely military rather than sentimental considerations would determine Israeli plans.

Although well before May small detachments of regular Arab troops were operating in Palestine, the real invasion began on the night of 14/15 May. On the morning of 15 May four regiments of the Arab Legion, under British officers, crossed the Allenby Bridge into Palestine, with Jerusalem as the ultimate objective and Nablus and Ramallah as immediate targets. In the south the Egyptian expeditionary force began to advance in two columns along the two available highways, one along the coast through Gaza and the other to the east toward Beersheba. The Lebanese force moved south along the coast, the Syrians came in from the east with the intention of occupying Galilee, and the Iraqis were to advance to the south of the Syrians with the aim of reaching the sea and thereby cutting the newly proclaimed state of Israel in half. Meanwhile the ALA and its 10,000 troops, with armed Arabs, prepared to defend Arab settlements while the Muslim Brotherhood force was, optimistically, expected to co-operate with the advancing Egyptians. On 15 May a radio broadcast by Ben-Gurion from Tel Aviv, explaining to Americans why the state of Israel had been proclaimed, was punctuated by bombs dropped from Egyptian aircraft.

Soon after the invasion the UN appointed a mediator, Count Bernadotte of Sweden, to whom the Israelis took an instant, perhaps calculated, dislike; he was alleged to be pro-British and pro-Nazi. But eventually a truce was arranged to begin on 11 June. In the intervening period of hostilities the invading armies discovered that the Israelis were not going to grant an easy victory, while the Israelis learned that, with the arrival of imported weapons, they were capable of beating off their attackers.

In the south, the Syrians failed to win the battle for the Jordan Valley. The key battle here was the Syrian attack on the two villages of Degania A and Degania B. The former was defended by 70 Israelis against Syrian infantry, artillery, armored cars and five tanks. The tanks broke

through to the inner Israeli trenches, where they were engaged with 'Molotov cocktails'; because the tanks outpaced the infantry, this attack failed, and the Syrians lost some tanks and armored cars. The attackers then sent eight tanks and armored cars against Degania B, but halfway through this battle the first field artillery imported by Israel arrived, and went into action with untrained crews. These guns

had little material effect, but their presence was sufficient to persuade the Syrians to withdraw. However, some days later the Jewish settlement of Mishmar Hayarden fell to Syrian armor despite a

BELOW: *Israeli troops in action, 1948.*
BOTTOM: *The armored cab of this Jewish truck provided little protection to its driver when caught in Arab sniper fire.*

desperate defense by Israeli infantry. On the eve of the truce, Israeli morale was restored when about 100 men and women successfully defended the settlement of Ein Gev against a Syrian battalion enjoying artillery support. On the other side of Galilee, the Lebanese were fairly unsuccessful, and in their retreats often abandoned weapons which were of great use to the ill-equipped Israeli forces.

In the center, Israel's narrow waistline, two Iraqi infantry brigades with an armored brigade in support struck west from Nablus and got within six miles of Natanya, on the Mediterranean coast, before being stopped by a *Palmach* brigade. The Israeli command then undertook an operation with three *Palmach* brigades to defeat this force. The key town and road junction of Jenin was the objective but, thanks to a paucity of Israeli artillery, the presence of hostile aircraft, and the failure of one brigade to attack as planned, the operation was a failure. When the truce came the Iraqis had been blocked, but were still in a threatening position.

Both sides fought keenly for Jerusalem

RIGHT: *Israel acquired three Boeing B-17 Flying Fortress bombers in 1948.*
BELOW: *A captured Syrian Somua tank.*

one bomber and three fighter squadrons, as well as Crusader tanks. Progressing village by village, their advance was slow, thanks to determined resistance by armed settlers. King Farouk had sent his forces partly to counteract the influence of King Abdullah, and partly to divert the attention of Egyptians from his domestic troubles. The poor performance of his army, however, promised scant achievement of these objectives. But on the eve of the truce the Egyptians secured the high ground commanding the Majdal-Faluja road, thereby cutting off the Negev from the rest of Israel.

themselves both materially and organizationally. With help from Jews living abroad, a considerable quantity of weapons had been purchased from a variety of countries, and this flow continued during the truce. In addition, Czechoslovakia was openly supplying arms, including some Messerschmitt fighter aircraft. Three Flying Fortress bombers had also been acquired, and in July these would manage to drop a few bombs on Cairo and Damascus. British-built Beaufighters also appeared. More important perhaps were the variegated collections of guns and armored vehicles that began to appear; they had

in this period. The Jewish part of that city, despite great shortages, especially of water, managed to hold out against the Arab Legion, while the Israeli forces suffered many casualties in successive assaults against Latrun, whose capture was expected to open the highway for supply convoys. Although Latrun remained in Arab hands, before the truce began the Israelis finished a diversionary road and this enabled them, in the truce period, to resupply Jewish Jerusalem.

In the south the comparatively well-equipped but not especially enthusiastic Egyptians moved up along the two classic invasion routes. They were supported by

This truce was set to last for four weeks, and its conditions were abused as far as possible by both sides. Most of the Arab armies were reinforced, but the dissent between their governments continued. King Abdullah, even though he was supreme commander of the Arab forces, was refused permission to visit the Egyptian Army headquarters; his suspected intention of adding the Arab parts of Palestine to his Kingdom of Transjordan still determined Egyptian attitudes toward him, and the circumstance that his Arab Legion had proved to be the most effective force fighting Israel did not make him less unpopular. The Israelis strengthened

been bought on the basis of availability rather than suitability, but they enabled the Israeli Army to undertake more sophisticated operations. Under new conscription acts, and with an influx of volunteers from abroad, the Israeli forces also grew quantitively.

The conscription act of May had also instituted the IDF (Israel Defense Forces), which was to be the only armed force. This meant the abolition of private armies like the IZL and Stern Gang. However, these did not disband willingly, and there was a bloody encounter in June, when the SS *Altelena*, loaded with recruits and arms for the IZL, arrived at Tel Aviv and, refusing to submit to the IDF, was thereupon sunk by the latter. Despite this incident, with its 15 deaths, this was not quite the end for the IZL, for it remained active in Jerusalem for a few more weeks.

Since both sides knew when the truce was due to end, they both were ready, and began hostilities a few hours before the set time. This next phase of the war was destined to last only nine days, and was marked by increased Israeli self-confidence. The *Haganah*, whose staff was now better co-ordinated, had four main aims: opening the Tel Aviv to Jerusalem highway; capturing the Old City of Jerusalem; inflicting a clear defeat on the Syrians by recapturing Mishmar Hayarden; and routing the ALA at Nazareth. Most of the fighting was therefore in the north and center, although there were sporadic engagements with the Egyptians in the south. In the center the fighting was

ABOVE: *A wounded Egyptian soldier, 1948.*

ABOVE: *Israelis salvage parts from an Egyptian Air Force Supermarine Spitfire fighter.*

hard, because *Palmach* and Arab Legion forces were at grips there.

The Israelis eventually captured Lydda (Lod) with its international airport, and Ramallah. In these operations they fielded an armored brigade (the 8th) of 10 French H35 light tanks supported by the two ex-British Army Cromwells. However, the Arab Legion at Latrun held out, in one spectacular assault on 14 July they destroyed with a single gun the entire Israeli armored support (five tanks of the 8th Armored Brigade). Latrun, commanding the road to Jerusalem, was still in Arab hands when the next truce came into force on 18 July. Thus the Israelis in this sector had not gained all their objectives, and nor did they capture Old Jerusalem, where there was bitter fighting. Against the Syrians they had been clearly unsuccessful. The Israelis' Operation *Barosh*, designed to recapture Mishmar Hayarden by converging attacks of four columns, failed, partly because successful advances were not exploited and partly because Syrian resistance was stronger than expected. Finally, the Syrians had been able to prepare a counterattack by two brigades from Mishmar Hayarden, and these pushed the Israelis back.

However, in Galilee the Israelis were more successful. Their Anglo-Saxon Brigade, whose two battalions were supported by a few tanks and armored cars and could carry a few of its companies in half-tracks and jeeps, moved southeast against Nazareth. Some stiff resistance was encountered along the road, but Nazareth was captured on 16 July, with Kaukji and his ALA staff escaping in time to save themselves but not the declining reputation of the ALA. The Israelis were also successful against the Egyptians. Toward the end of the nine-day hostilities they could spare a *Palmach* battle group for this front and the Egyptians were pushed out of several settlements. In this sector, the costly

failure of repeated Egyptian assaults on Negba and Beerot Yitzhak seems to have finally broken the fighting spirit of the Egyptian expeditionary force, which henceforth displayed an essentially defensive mentality. In general the Egyptians, like the other Arab regular armies except for the Arab Legion, were more successful in defense than in attack. This may be because attack produces the kind of unexpected situation which demands self-confident problem-solving by junior officers, an ability in short supply when the population from which an army is drawn is educationally deprived.

The truce which began on 18 July was virtually imposed by international pressure expressed through the United Nations. Unlike the previous truce, it had no set duration and is regarded as having lasted until 18 October, although within this period there were several outbreaks of fighting as one or the other side tried to improve its position. In this summer, Count Bernadotte and his assistants tried to construct a new mutually acceptable partition plan, in which the Negev would be allocated to the Arabs and in return all of Galilee would be absorbed by Israel. The Arabs rejected these suggestions, largely because King Abdullah's Transjordan seemed likely to be the chief beneficiary, with lands allotted to the Arabs eventually becoming part of that Kingdom. Israel rejected the proposals not so much because it did not wish to lose the Negev but because the main achievement of its enemies during the previous months had been to show Israel how strong it was. Israel's position was now much improved; its army had held its own even before the new weapons flowed in, while the unexpected exodus of so much of the Arab population opened a new perspective for the creation of a homogenous Jewish state in which few concessions needed to be offered to the non-Jewish population.

Influential forces had, ever since the arrival of Bernadotte, conducted against him what in later years would be termed a smear campaign; evidently he was not regarded as a man who would unduly favor the Jews. In September, while driving in a part of Jerusalem regarded as neutral and international, his car was ambushed and he was killed. His assailants are believed to have been members of the Stern Gang or IZL, but the Israeli government's investigation of the crime never produced results. This lack of success was not because, as critics alleged, the government did not wish to pursue the murderers but rather because Israelis who knew something of the matter solidly refused to provide information. However, the government did disband the IZL, which had survived in Jerusalem. Bernadotte was succeeded as UN mediator by the American Ralph Bunche, who was unable to avert a reopening of hostilities in October.

Full-scale hostilities were recommenced by the Israelis, against the Egyptians, on 15 October. However, Israel could claim that Egyptian interference with an Israeli supply convoy, sent to the Negev under UN auspices, had been a provocation. In this southern sector the initial Israeli aim was to secure a route by which the Negev could be reconnected with the rest of the country: all the main roads were blocked by the Egyptians at this period. Colonel Allon commanded a force of about 15,000 men for this operation, and they faced about the same number of Egyptians. The latter were astride the two roads leading from Sinai northward and in addition, around Faluja, they commanded the east-west Majdal–Hebron road linking these two routes. In late September, during the truce, the Israeli forces had captured a few heights which would aid them in this project, Operation 'Ten Plagues.' As soon as the Egyptians, as expected, fired on the Israeli supply column on 15 October, the Israeli Air Force attacked Egyptian airfields in the Negev and thereby gained control of the air. Israeli forces then attacked the east-west road at several points and also managed to bring the north-south coast road under artillery fire. A substantial attack was made on Iraq el Manshiya but this, like several other attacks made on this road, was beaten off by strong Egyptian defenses. It was not until 20 October that Allon, having changed the direction of his attack, captured Huleiqat and thereby opened up a route to the Negev. When the Israelis captured Beersheba, cutting off Egyptian forces along the Beersheba–Hebron road, Arab Legion units were sent to Hebron to help; this was the only occasion in these weeks when other Arab armies went to help the hard-pressed Egyptians.

When the Egyptian strongpoint of Beit Hanun on the coast road fell to an Israeli attack, the Egyptian forces on the coast road to the north were threatened with isolation, and they were accordingly withdrawn. This left a pocket of Egyptian forces astride the east-west road around Faluja. Although the Israelis captured Iraq Suedan at the west end of this pocket the Egyptian commander, Said Taha Bey, at a meeting with Allon, refused terms of honorable surrender (leading Allon to comment that his Egyptian opponent was a braver man than the Egyptian government deserved). In fact the Faluja Pocket held out until an armistice was signed between Israel and Egypt, and its defenders then marched out with full military honors.

A new and very mobile campaign had been launched by Allon against the Egyptians in December. They were still tied to the two main roads in the Negev, being unwilling to risk cross-country movements. Operation *Horev* was based on the assumption that the Egyptians were very strong in the Gaza area and would inflict heavy losses in a frontal attack. Accordingly, the Israeli attack would be against the lateral link between their eastern and western forces. The Egyptians on the eastern road were to be pushed back, and then the advancing Israelis would swing westward and later northward to advance on El Arish, well inside Egyptian territory.

The Israelis did begin with an attack toward Gaza, but this was only a diversion. In the east they had cleared an old Roman road of centuries-old sand and debris and used this to by-pass the Egyptian strongpoints located along the parallel, newer, highway. In this way they reached El Anja, which they shortly captured. Allon then split his forces, sending some along the road westward to Rafah and others into Egyptian territory toward El Arish via Abu Ageila. Despite Egyptian appeals, fraternal Arab armies made no attempt to attack Israel from other directions to relieve the pressure. It was the British who proved to be the temporary saviors of the Egyptian regime; they informed Israel that, in accordance with the 1936 Anglo-Egyptian Treaty, Britain would have to intervene if Israeli forces remained on Egyptian soil. So in early January the attack on El Arish was called off and Israeli forces were withdrawn from Sinai; Allon had decided to concentrate on the capture of Rafah, but before the city could be taken the Egyptians signed an armistice. Israel's willingness to sign was enhanced by her deteriorating international position after British fighters, patrolling the Sinai-Israel frontier, had been shot down by Israeli aircraft.

The only other scene of considerable

ABOVE: *Izaak Bey Dessouky, the Egyptian commander of Gaza.*

fighting in this final phase of the war was in Galilee, where the Israelis decided to put an end to the ALA. The essence of Operation *Hiram* was a pincer movement closing on Sasa, one arm moving westward from Safed and the other eastward from Kabiri. Sasa was close to the Lebanese frontier and the closing of the pincers would cut off Kaukji's ALA, which was located to the south. Another Israeli thrust from the south toward Sasa would then destroy the ALA. The operations lasted from 28–31 October and, apart from a short hold-up caused by stiff resistance at Tarshiha, went according to plan. The ALA was finally destroyed, losing about 400 dead and 500 prisoners, and the Israelis advanced to occupy a strip of Lebanese territory up to the Litani River, an advance made purely for bargaining purposes.

ABOVE: *Defenders of Kibbutz Negba in the Negev armed with a Bren light machine gun and Lee Enfield rifles.*
LEFT: *Israeli troops advance under fire.*

Arab residents of El Majdal in the Negev, Palestine, watch impassively as Israeli troops occupy the city, 13 November 1948.

UNEASY TRUCE

The net result of the war of 1948, started by the Arabs to stifle Israel at birth, was a quite unexpected enlargement and strengthening of the new Jewish state. The war had not only witnessed the creation of the Israel Defense Force, but the IDF's increasing battleworthiness had ensured that the frontiers of Israel, temporary though they might be, had advanced well beyond the limits envisaged in the UN partition plan whose implementation had first provoked the Arab assault. This new capability and new expansion was emphasized on the eve of the truce with Jordan, when an IDF detachment pushed south to the Gulf of Aqaba to plant the Israeli flag near the site of what would later be the port of Eilat.

Meanwhile the Arabs of the territory occupied by Israel, who once had formed an overwhelming majority of the population, had largely disappeared. There were now two refugee problems, 800,000 Jews who had been expelled from Arab countries, and the 800,000 or so displaced Arabs of Palestine, who by 1949 were distributed in camps in Lebanon, Syria, Jordan and the south Palestine coastal strip (the Gaza Strip) which the Egyptians had managed to retain. The Palestinian refugees hoped, and were told by their host governments, that they would soon return. They were not encouraged to make new lives for themselves in their new countries, and there seems little doubt that Israel's enemies regarded these refugees as a powerful weapon. Concentrated in primitive camps near Israel's frontiers, having little to do apart from cultivating their understandable grievances against the Jews who had dispossessed them, they served as a reminder to the world that Israel, founded to undo an ancient wrong, had resulted in a new injustice. From the ranks of the first, second, and then third generation of these homeless people would come bitter and uncompromising recruits for an armed struggle against Israel, in which Arab governments would also participate. The armistices signed in 1948–49 were not treaties and did not recognize Israel's right to exist.

Whatever the wrongs caused by the creation of Israel, the continued suffering of the dispossessed Palestinians was largely a result of, at best, Arab neglect or, at worst, cynical Arab manipulation. That part of international opinion that was not prejudiced by the pursuit of its own interests could only view the situation with compassionate alarm, while striving unsuccessfully to reconcile Arab with Jew and helping the refugees with funds which the Arab governments themselves seemed reluctant to contribute. Feeling for the ancient Jewish predicament and growing admiration for what the Israelis were achieving conflicted with knowledge of the refugee camps, where families dispossessed of land held for centuries by their ancestors festered in poverty and idleness. In this sense the creation of Israel could be regarded as a triumph of sentiment over morality.

All in all, the policies of the Arab leaders in this period were characterized by an ineptitude that could not be compensated by their unscrupulousness. This incompetence was not unremarked by the more perceptive of their citizens, and a consequence was that the leaders of the 1948 fiasco against Israel were, sooner or later, deposed and sometimes murdered by their own irate people. One of the first to go was the Egyptian prime minister, assassinated in December 1948 when it became obvious that, despite all the bluster, the Egyptian expeditionary force faced defeat. In 1952 King Farouk was himself deposed by a group of army officers whose most effective member was Gamal Nasser, who had begun to turn his thoughts toward conspiracy while commanding a unit in the Faluja Pocket. As soon as the war was over one of the more successful Syrian generals, Hasni el Zaim, who had commanded the armored brigade at the battle of Mishmar Hayarden, overthrew the government but was himself overthrown two years later. In Iraq, the Hashemite monarchy survived, partly owing to the support received from its patron, Britain. It was not until after Britain had sacrificed its reputation among Arabs by the 1956 Suez campaign that the royal regime in Iraq would meet its bloody end.

The case of King Abdullah, murdered in 1951, was a little different. His troops had done better than the other Arab forces in 1948, and Transjordan had been enlarged by the conflict; at a ceremony in Jericho, he had been proclaimed king of a new state, the Hashemite Kingdom of Jordan, which was formed by joining Arab Palestine (the 'West Bank') with Transjordan. Partly because he was a beneficiary of the situation, but partly because he had a more flexible view, Abdullah was prepared to concede the existence of Israel. Rumors that he was about to sign an agreement with the Jews led to his assassination by religious zealots

LEFT: *Arab inhabitants of El Faluja are evacuated to Gaza under UN supervision.*

is a philosophy which is understandable in the situation in which Israel found itself, but it was usually the wrong eye and the wrong tooth.

In the early 1950s the Israeli reprisal raids were often ineffective and sometimes accompanied by disproportionate casualties. In other cases, the Israeli units retired to their own frontiers as soon as they came under fire. It seemed that the spirit of 1948 had disappeared from the IDF. Moshe Dayan, who was Chief of Staff from 1953, made several changes to remedy this situation. He made it clear to his operation officers that not until a unit had suffered 50 percent casualties would a change or abandonment of a mission become acceptable, and any officer failing to observe this new ruling would put his career in danger. A little earlier, an elite unit known as Force 101 had been formed under the leadership of Ariel ('Arik') Sharon, a former intelligence officer. Composed of the more intelligent and better

LEFT: *Israelis at morning prayers behind their barricades at Kfar Etzion, 1949.*
BELOW: *Peace comes to Safed, 1949.*

on the steps of the El Aqsa mosque in Jerusalem. His grandson Hussein succeeded him a year later, and managed to retain control in the turbulent years that followed. One of his early moves was the dismissal of Glubb Pasha; at the time this was portrayed in the West as resulting from pressure from Nasser, but was probably no more than a recognition that Glubb Pasha had, by force of circumstances, become far too powerful.

Although operations in the 1948 war had been on a small scale, there was hardly a day which did not witness an engagement of some kind, so total casualties were quite substantial. Israel lost 6000 killed, of whom about 2000 were civilians. The Arabs lost rather more, but no reliable figures have been published for their total losses. The armistices of 1949 did not bring an end to casualties, for the occasional incident occurred, and guerrilla activities (Arab description) or terrorist attacks (Israeli description) slowly intensified. By 1955 there was an annual total of 250 Israeli civilians killed or wounded in these attacks. The Arab term for the attackers was *Fedayeen*, an ancient word describing commando-style forces used for suicide squads. The new *Fedayeen* began with sabotage and swift incursions across the frontiers and, in common with most terrorist-style guerrillas, found that the murder of civilians was the safest and most attention-gaining activity. At first, such raids were sporadic, born of a natural hatred of the Israelis on the part of frustrated and embittered individuals. Later, the raids were better organized by Palestinian 'liberation' groups, and helped or encouraged by various Arab governments.

The Israeli Defense Forces found that they were unable to anticipate these attacks. The only defense, and it was burdensome and not highly effective, was the maintenance of armed home-guard arrangements in the most vulnerable areas. As a matter of policy, the IDF was entrusted with retaliatory attacks across the frontiers in response to *Fedayeen* actions. Although these IDF ventures were habitually described as hitting back at terrorist bases, in reality they hurt the innocent most of all. An eye for an eye and a tooth for a tooth

educated conscripts, its original role had been as a volunteer unit for making raids across the frontiers. Dayan had had some misgivings about this unit, because he believed that the essential problem was not the mounting of successful reprisal raids, but the improvement of morale from top to bottom in the army. However, this unit of picked men, by setting an example, did in fact do much to raise the spirit and competence of the army as a whole. In 1954, just half a year after its formation, Force 101 was merged with the paratroops, with Sharon becoming commander of the Paratroop Battalion. For a few months the Paratroops were entrusted with the cross-border operations, and soon established a record of daring and technical competence. Other units did their best to emulate the paratroopers, and it was not long before a number of them reached a standard which enabled them to take over some of the paratroopers' work in reprisal operations.

During the early 1950s the IDF developed into a force which, man for man, was the most effective of its time. It was largely a civilian army based on a conscription system that was later stabilized at three years service for males and two years for women. Christians and Muslims could serve, but only as volunteers, while Druzes were conscripted under the same terms as Jews. Women stayed on the reserve only until the age of 25, but men stayed until their mid-50s. Because, over the years, the ex-conscript reserves accumulated, the IDF became a force with a small regular nucleus and a disproportionately large reserve. General Yigael

RIGHT: *Israeli officers confer with United Nations observers at Gaza in 1949.*
BELOW: *Colonel Moshe Dayan and his staff watch Israel Defense Force maneuvers.*

Yadin, the IDF's second Chief of Staff, was largely responsible for the system of very rapid mobilization of reserves; a rapidity which more than once confounded Israel's enemies, and was less a consequence of Israel's small size and good communications than of very thorough and intelligent planning, together with a readiness to co-operate on the part of the whole Jewish population. After the 1956 war the nature of the IDF attracted worldwide attention; while newspapers at one end of the market published photographs of strapping women soldiers, the more serious observers studied the army's mobilization procedures. The careful combination of informality and efficiency was less publicized, even though it was the most innovative and significant feature of the IDF. The circumstances of Israel – its small population, fragile economy, and con-

tinuing peril – meant that the IDF had no time for pomp, or other aspects of military life unconnected with effectiveness as a weapon. The IDF was a war machine, to be maintained in good order but not to be kept in daily use. By the 1980s its capability was so great that some observers, not always with the best of motives, likened it to the German *Wehrmacht*. This analogy is misleading, for while the IDF was organized with German thoroughness and comprised a well-educated, well-trained and enterprising soldiery, it did not need the *Wehrmacht*'s style of discipline. The 1948 war had been won, despite somewhat mediocre Israeli generalship, by the excellence of the middle-ranking and junior officers and the devotion of the soldiers. In the period after 1948 it was the successful and popular majors, captains, and colonels who climbed to the rank of gen-

ABOVE: *An IDF Air Force Meteor F8.*
RIGHT: *Israeli Mosquito Mk VI fighter-bombers.*

eral and, in some cases, to Minister of Defense. The mediocrities and disciplinarians tended to fade away.

Predestined to fight in a situation of numerical disadvantage both in personnel and weapons, with the likelihood of a war on several fronts, the IDF developed a military philosophy which cultivated innovation and flexibility. Night operations, in which numerical disparity is less important, became an Israeli speciality in 1948, and remained so. Speed of movement, especially off the roads, was emphasized. This enabled forces to be switched from theater to theater and to gain the advantage of surprise.

In 1948 the IDF managed to acquire a few weapons from abroad, but its equipment was plainly inadequate; even at the end of the war its most effective ground-attack aircraft were the slow Austers, ex-British machines equipped to drop a light bomb. But the IDF's air force entered the 1956 war with jet aircraft which, although early models, were capable of effective use. Meteor fighters had been obtained from Britain, and Ouragans, Vautours, and the more modern Mystère IVs from France. US DC3 (Dakota) piston-engined aircraft were used not only for transport but as drop aircraft for the well-equipped paratroop

LEFT: *Soldiers of the Arab Legion man a 40mm Bofors antiaircraft gun.*
BELOW LEFT: *An armored car regiment of the Arab Legion parades with hawk mascot, 1953.*

Nasser, who became president of Egypt, had great ambitions which led him into two wars with Israel, in 1956 and 1967. These wars detracted from his record as a leader who did much to rescue his countrymen from the social and economic neglect suffered under Farouk, but hardly damaged his popularity. He was in any case a true Arab nationalist, although his desire to make Egypt, and himself, dominant in the Arab world, encouraged him to exploit the quarrel with Israel in ways that were not always to the ultimate benefit of the Arabs.

A necessary step for Nasser's ambition was the creation of a new and battleworthy army. In 1955, soon after the British had agreed to withdraw from their bases along the Suez Canal (in effect bringing to an end Britain's military presence in Egypt), Nasser made a definite swing from Egypt's Western orientation by concluding an arms agreement with Czechoslovakia. Since Czechoslovakia was part of the Soviet bloc, the effect of this was to obtain Soviet weapons for the Egyptian forces. Nasser openly and deliberately announced this as a step toward the destruction of Israel, thereby enhancing his reputation among Arabs of all countries as the man most likely to achieve that obsessional ambition. This transaction alarmed the Western powers not so much because of the threat to Israel as because it opened the way to Soviet involvement in the Middle East. Egypt bought 230 Soviet tanks, 200 armored personnel carriers, 100 self-propelled guns and 500 other guns for the Egyptian Army. The Air Force received MiG-15 fighters to supplement its older British-built Vampires, while the Navy was re-created with the acquisition of two Soviet destroyers and some submarines. Ideally, a year or two should have been allowed for the Egyptian forces to master these new weapons, both technically and tactically. However Nasser, not for the last time, was overimpatient and found himself at war with Israel before the new weapons had been thoroughly assimilated.

While accumulating weapons, Nasser attempted to discomfit Israel while enhancing his popular backing in the Arab world. He gave his support to the *Fedayeen* raids in Israel, and supported radical movements in Africa and the Middle East. In 1954 it may have been his inspiration which lay behind the anti-Western riots in Jordan. He also helped the Algerian revolutionary movement (FLN) against the French. This decision serves as a good example of the way in which his impatience tended to override political caution; by helping an anti-French movement he

brigade. The army was equipped with a variety of tanks, including French AMX light tanks, and US Sherman and Super Sherman medium tanks. Available guns included the well-tried British 25-pounder, 105mm self-propelled guns, various anti-tank guns, and 120mm mortars. The infantry was quite mobile, having 6 × 6 motor trucks, and enough half-track personnel carriers to make swift battlefield deployment of large units a frequent feature of Israeli tactics. Only the IDF

navy, whose role was necessarily secondary, lagged behind. It had a couple of ex-British destroyers, but little else.

Israel's main enemy in the 1956 war was Egypt, which under Nasser's leadership was plainly the leading Arab state in terms of the continuing struggle against the existence of a Jewish state in the Middle East. Because the Farouk regime had been so uncompromisingly hostile, the Israelis greeted the Egyptian officers' new government with some hope. But

brought France and Israel closer together, facilitating, among other things, Israel's purchase of French weapons like the Mystère fighters that were to prove so decisive in the 1956 war.

Where he could control international waterways, Nasser blocked the passage of Israeli shipping. This was contrary to United Nations resolutions, but the case against him in international law was probably not as strong as the Western powers claimed. Here too, the gain seemed small in comparison to the loss of international goodwill, but Nasser placed a great, possibly inflated, value on his popularity with the Arab masses. As well as blocking the Suez Canal to Israeli ships and ships trading with Israel, Nasser installed artillery at Ras Nasrani, which prevented Israel-bound ships passing the Strait of Tiran en route to the port of Eilat.

In October 1955 the forces of Syria and Egypt were placed under joint command, obviously in anticipation of some action against Israel. Some months later Jordan was also persuaded to join this arrangement. In early 1956 the Israeli government, still headed by Ben-Gurion, concluded that Nasser's hostile stance was not merely a question of image and propaganda, but was preparation for war. In July the IDF general staff began to plan for an imminent war whose precise timing and nature could only be guessed at.

BELOW: *An Egyptian T34/85 tank in the Sinai, 1956.*

ABOVE: *Israeli Prime Minister Moshe Sharett.*

BELOW: *Israeli AMX 13 tanks withdraw from the Gaza Strip, 8 March 1957. UN forces took control of the area.*

SUEZ AND SINAI
—1956—

The conflict of 1956 is rarely described as a war; the Israelis prefer to term it the Sinai Campaign, while the French and British refer to it as the Suez Affair. There are good reasons for this. The Israeli forces, which started the action, took care not to engage in a full-scale war against the territory of Egypt but concentrated on defeating its armed forces and breaking the blockade of the southern port of Eilat. For their part, the French and British governments, aware from the very first days that they faced catastrophic failure, did all they could to minimize the significance of this war, and avoidance of the term war was one part of this public relations effort; British ministers aroused some hilarity in the Houses of Parliament by insisting on calling it, rather euphemistically, a 'state of armed conflict.'

What each of the warring governments told the world and their own people during and after the war was a mixture of fact and falsehood. On the whole the Israeli and French governments stuck close to the truth, or at least preferred reticence to falsehood; Nasser and his supporters indulged in sheer propaganda which, however, had a factual foundation; while the British government, goaded perhaps by a press which was persistent and sometimes hostile, gave a clean account of the hostilities, but lied both to the British people and to Parliament on the subject of its motives and preparations for this war.

Partly because of the reluctance of those who knew what happened in London and Paris in October 1956 to give a clear and clean account of the negotiations which preceded the Israeli and Anglo-French attacks on Egypt (a reluctance which in the British case went as far as denying that certain key negotiations had ever taken place), the preliminaries of this war are in some ways more interesting than the war itself. Moshe Dayan, as Israeli Chief of Staff, took part in some of these negotiations. Dayan was not quite the simple honest soldier which many Israelis believe he was, but his description of what happened at the meetings he attended does seem simple and honest, while his speculations about what happened in his absence, while less reliable, make intelligent use of whatever facts he was able to glean.

There can be little doubt that this war was provoked by President Nasser of Egypt; indeed Nasser himself took care to emphasize this, as one more fact to enhance his popularity among the masses, not only of his own country but throughout the Arab world. There is little doubt, too, of Nasser's sincerity in his wish to avenge the humiliation of the 1948 war and of his sense of the injustice that had been perpetrated against the Palestinians. On the other hand his desire for greatness, both for Egypt and himself, led him into actions that produced more applause than

tangible gain. The 1956 war followed this pattern, for although the Israelis clearly defeated the Egyptians, the spectacular humiliation of the Franco-British intervention was sufficient to divert attention from the fact that Nasser had provoked a war against Israel in which he had been defeated.

At the end of July 1956 Nasser addressed a huge crowd of his supporters in Cairo and produced tumultuous applause by announcing the nationalization of the Anglo-French Suez Canal Company. Although the possibility of financial compensation was not excluded, London and Paris were shaken by this move. In Britain, it was a received truth, emphasized by the strategies of two world wars, that the Suez Canal was the main artery of the British Empire. The prospect of the Canal being operated (and hence controlled) by Egyptians was quite unpalatable to politicians as well as to the public and most of the press.

The British prime minister by this time was Anthony Eden, whose reputation considerably exceeded his capability. In the 1930s, as foreign secretary, Eden had been so irritated by his prime minister's interference in the making of foreign policy that he had resigned in protest. As the immediate disagreement between him and Prime Minister Chamberlain had been about the correct attitude to adopt toward Mussolini and Hitler, Eden gained, justifiably but accidentally, the reputation of being the man who had stood up to the dictators. This, with hard work, and his personal attractiveness, had been the foundation of his subsequent political success. But underneath his suave exterior was a well-hidden excitability of character, and by 1956 this had been heightened by an irritating ailment which inevitably took a turn for the worse at times of tension.

Having built his career on opposition to Hitler and Mussolini, it is hardly surprising that Eden began to see parallels between Nasser and Hitler; as things turned out, his inability to see the difference between an ex-corporal of the German Army and an ex-colonel of the Egyptian Army brought his downfall. Eden was determined to overthrow Nasser in one way or another; whether the nationalization of the Suez Canal confirmed him in this view, or whether its importance lay in its providing a pretext for military action, is not clear and probably never will be. Until Nasser began to obsess him, Eden had tended to be pro-Arab. His understanding that British strategy was based on friendship with, especially, Jordan and Iraq, was one reason for this, but he also had a genuine sympathy for the displaced Palestinians.

Inside the British cabinet Eden was probably the most hostile to Nasser. Those who would support him through thick and thin were probably in a minority. A few were definitely against any military adventure, while the majority, understandably, could not make up their minds. In the French cabinet there appears to have been somewhat more determination to put an end to Nasser even though Prime Minister Mollet was not a man of strong character. Nasser's blatant support for the Algerian Arabs, who at the time were fighting for independence from France, was probably the main motive for the French reaction although, with its interests in Indo-China, France also regarded the Suez Canal as an important means of communication with its overseas territories.

For Israel, the nationalization of the Canal represented both a threat and a

BELOW: *An Egyptian Air Force MiG-15 is examined by Israeli technicians, 1956.*

Israeli officers, in Paris to discuss arms purchases, were the first to feel a warmer relationship developing after the nationalization. They were asked by the French Defense Ministry whether they could supply Israeli intelligence appreciations of the size and disposition of the Egyptian forces. Meanwhile the British and French governments were conferring about what steps should be taken to resist the nationalization. The first formal meeting was in London and seems to have resulted in a decision to prepare a military operation aimed at securing the Suez Canal Zone and restoring the status quo. It was assumed, with some pleasure, that this operation would also result in the overthrow of Nasser by his own disillusioned people or army. The British territories of Malta and Cyprus were to be the Mediterranean

ABOVE: *President Nasser and Anthony Nutting sign the treaty ending British control of the Suez Canal in Cairo in 1954.*
RIGHT: *Eden (left), his wife and Selwyn Lloyd, 26 September 1956.*

promise. A threat, because a successful outcome of this venture would enhance Nasser's prestige and hence his power, a power which he was obviously only too anxious to employ in the destruction of Israel. It was a promise because by turning Britain and France against Egypt it created the possibility that, in a future war against Egypt, Israel would not fight alone. More immediately, it seemed likely that procurement of arms from Britain and France would become easier. Hitherto, while Nasser was engaged in re-equipping his forces with Russian weapons, Britain, France and the USA had been reluctant to grant licenses for the export of military equipment to Israel. Ostensibly, this was on the grounds that such shipments would exacerbate tension in the Middle East, but in reality the reluctance was maintained because the Western powers were anxious to improve their relationships with the Arab countries. On the eve of the Canal nationalization Israel was obtaining arms only from France, and these in very limited numbers. Twelve Mystère jet fighters, somewhat superior to the MIG types flown by the Egyptians, were being delivered, but the French foreign ministry was trying to persuade Mollet to halt further shipments. The AMX light tanks and the secondhand Sherman tanks expected from France were also threatened; however an Israeli delegation hurriedly dispatched to Paris in June had extracted promises of a more liberal policy; Nasser's interference in 'French internal affairs' (his support of the Algerian rebels) was probably the most powerful argument against those who felt French arms should be withheld in the interests of good relations with Egypt. At about the same time, Britain agreed to let Israel buy some

Meteor night fighters; only six aircraft were involved, but they were badly needed, and there was a probability that more might follow. All the same, despite these easings in the summer of 1956, Israel was still severely restricted in its arms procurement and its numerical deficiency in modern weaponry when compared to Egypt was alarming. Nevertheless, Dayan believed that even with the weapons available the Israelis could defeat the Egyptians, and he recommended an immediate attack on Nasser's forces while the Western world was still shaken by the nationalization announcement. Israel, he said, could overrun the Sinai Peninsula up to the Canal and re-establish international control over the waterway. However, Ben-Gurion was most reluctant to make war; his objection that Israel lacked weapons was a good argument, but was probably secondary in his mind to a feeling that the risks were clear while the promised gains might not be forthcoming if premature action by Israel alienated world opinion.

bases for this operation, code-named 'Musketeer.' It would be commanded by a British general (Sir Charles Keightley), with a French admiral (Pierre Barjot) as deputy.

It was apparently Admiral Barjot who suggested that the Anglo-French operation might be assisted by Israeli co-operation, and the Israeli military attaché was soon informed of this. The first formal Franco-Israeli discussions came in early September, when the Israeli Chief of Operations (the immediate subordinate of the Chief of Staff) met Admiral Barjot in Paris. This was followed by several other meetings, always held secretly in private houses even, later, when French, British and Israeli ministers attended. Later in the month Shimon Peres, then an official of the Israeli Defense Ministry, used a visit to Paris in connection with arms purchases to exploit his friendly relationships with leading French ministers and reach a common understanding about possible Israeli-French political

one occasion the Arab Legion was believed to have been involved. Moreover, some of the attacks seemed to have been accompanied by unnecessary cruelty, including the murder and mutilation of an Israeli girl. In the end it was decided to stage a larger than normal retributive attack, an Arab Legion fort just inside Jordan being selected as the target. Although the Israeli commando unit sent on this mission succeeded in capturing and then blowing up this fort, it did so only at the expense of high casualties. The result was a review of the policy of retributive strikes, which brought no comfort. Such strikes, it seemed, were not damaging enough to persuade King Hussein of Jordan to brave his enemies and forbid terrorist activities launched from Jordanian territory. Moreover, the Israeli incursions were always made in the most unfavorable conditions, for they had to traverse difficult country in

LEFT: *Keightley and Barjot.*
BELOW: *Golda Meir was Minister of Foreign Affairs in 1956.*

darkness while their enemy, knowing what inevitably followed a *Fedayeen* attack, was on the alert and ready to open fire. The casualties were especially worrying because it was elite units which undertook these operations and their soldiers were accordingly of more than ordinary value.

These conclusions provided an additional argument for those, like Dayan, who wanted a prompt full-scale battle. Only by inflicting a thorough military defeat on Egypt, it was thought, would the Israeli frontiers be guaranteed a more peaceful future, for a weakening of Nasser would inevitably entail a weakening of the *Fedayeen* whose activities he so energetically promoted. However, although this was a powerful emotional argument it was secondary to the feeling that since Nasser was proclaiming his intention of destroying Israel, and his forces were assimilating ever increasing inflows of Soviet weapons, it would be better for Israel to strike sooner rather than await an onslaught later.

As for the vital interests of Israel, ad-

co-operation in the Middle East. These talks were unofficial, but in fact proved to be very influential. Because the British, wishing to give an American peace initiative enough rope to hang itself, had decided to defer operation 'Musketeer,' the possibility of Franco-Israeli military operations, without the British, was discussed, and as a result Ben-Gurion agreed to act with France if necessary. When informed of this possibility, Eden implied that Britain would not object to a Franco-Israeli operation, provided Jordan was not attacked (current British treaty commitments to Jordan meant that if Jordan was attacked in a full-scale war by Israel, Britain would be obliged to go to its help).

Meanwhile, the rapidly developing situation caused the Israeli government to study, yet again, where its vital interests really lay. Failure to do this would have presented the possibility that it would be persuaded into a course of action which would benefit Britain and France more than itself. The negotiations in Paris at this time were only occupying part of the attention of the Israeli government; on the one hand it was not at all certain they would lead anywhere, except perhaps to an improvement in the arms supply situation, while on the other hand events nearer home were agitating the Israeli population. These events were a renewal of *Fedayeen* activity, undertaken by raiders operating from Jordanian territory. Such raiders were regarded by Israelis as Nasser's men, for the Jordanian government was under severe pressure from Nasserites to tolerate their activities, even though each raid was followed almost inevitably by Israeli retribution against Jordanian targets. In mid-September there was a surge of such *Fedayeen* activity, and on at least

ditional to the disarming of the military threat from Egypt, the one of most concern was control of the Straits of Tiran at the outlet of the Gulf of Aqaba. These Straits controlled access to the port of Eilat which, if operating freely, would not only permit the economic development of the Negev but also provide a port which to some extent might nullify any blockage of the Suez Canal to Israel shipping. The conquest of the Gaza Strip, although tempting when studied on a map, was regarded as not worth the trouble, given its population of hostile Arabs, many of them resentful Palestinians. Nor was the occupation of the whole of Sinai very attractive; it would certainly have provided a wide buffer zone between Egypt and Israel, but defending it seemed beyond the possibilities of the peacetime IDF.

In essence then, as negotiations with

RIGHT: *Ben-Gurion confers with Harry Truman and Abba Eban looks on.*
BELOW: *Lavon was Minister of Defense.*

the French progressed, the Israeli representatives kept in the center of their attention the chances of inflicting a drastic military defeat on Egypt, and regaining control of the Tiran Straits (which in effect meant control of Sharm el-Sheikh, where Egyptian artillery was currently installed).

At the end of September an Israeli delegation, including Foreign Minister Golda Meir, the Minister of Transport, the director-general of the Defense Ministry Shimon Peres, (Ben-Gurion being titular Minister of Defense), and Dayan met a corresponding French group in a private house in Paris. The French Foreign Minister (Pineau), asked whether Israel would join with France in military action against Egypt in the event of Britain withdrawing from its previous undertaking to co-operate with France. Despite American opposition to such an operation, which Pineau ascribed to US anxiety to pursue a more relaxed relationship with the USSR, the French believed that the

Canal nationalization showed that Nasser would have to be dealt with by force, and October was the best month for such an operation. Not only was this the last month of the year when the Mediterranean could be expected to be calm enough for landing operations, but it was the eve of the US presidential election and Eisenhower, the most likely victor, would hardly wish to lay himself open to the accusation that he was opposing America's allies for the sake of US-Soviet relations. Moreover, the USSR was itself preoccupied with popular discontent in Poland and Hungary and would therefore be unlikely to interfere in the Middle East. The Israeli response to this idea was favorable, subject to some reservations. In particular, Israel had to be certain that Britain would not go to the aid of Jordan if the latter intervened, and that the USA would not take economic measures against Israel in order to force an abandonment of the operation.

When these talks moved on to the technical aspects of the proposed operation it became clear that without Britain there would be no significant bomber force at the disposition of the invaders. Also, since Malta and Cyprus would not be available, the French Air Force might need to use Israeli bases. When the Israeli delegation returned home it was accompanied by French officers who were to examine the proposed bases and also report on the capability and needs of the Israeli forces. The report they sent to Paris recommended the supply of weapons, especially tanks and personnel carriers, and trucks suitable for desert conditions. Apparently they accepted the Israeli contention that the IDF was already strong enough and spirited enough to defeat the Egyptians singlehanded, the main obstacle to a

successful campaign being not the Egyptian Army but the desert and its hindrance to military transport.

On 2 October Dayan was able to inform his general staff that a campaign with the French, and possibly with the British, was likely, and would probably start on 20 October. Reserves would be mobilized only at the last minute so as to preserve secrecy, and military moves would be presented as directed against Jordan, which apart from harboring *Fedayeen* was also, it seemed, on the verge of accepting the stationing of Iraqi troops on its soil. The task of the IDF would be to capture the Sinai Peninsula while the French or Franco-British forces would occupy the Canal Zone and bomb the Egyptian airfields.

Ben-Gurion, however, was less eager than Dayan, and his was the decisive voice. In the absence of British bombers, he feared, Egyptian airfields would continue to function and enable Egyptian aircraft to bomb Israeli cities. With its frontline commitments, and disposing of only 70 Mystère, Ouragan, and Meteor aircraft, the Israeli Air Force would not be able to defend the town populations. Ben-Gurion also questioned the French assumption that, merely by occupying the Canal Zone, the French would secure the overthrow of Nasser. The Prime Minister was confident that the military action would result in Israeli victories, but he was not satisfied about the assumptions concerning how the war would start, and how it would end. But although a definite decision to act with the French was not taken, the French agreed to ship new weapons to Israel, while the Israeli staffs made preparations for the likely, but not inevitable, war with the Arab nations.

In mid-October there was a renewal of *Fedayeen* activity from Jordan, and another retributive raid was launched against a Jordanian Arab Legion fort. This was successful, but again there were substantial casualties. The renewed tension with Jordan did, however, enable Israeli preparations for war with Egypt to be passed off as preparations for a large-scale retributive raid against Jordan. The raid against the fort, at Kalkilia, led to King Hussein asking for British air support for the Arab Legion in accordance with Britain's treaty obligations; the British

government thereupon informed the Israeli government that Iraqi troops were about to take up station in Jordan and that if Israel took military action in response to this move Britain would be compelled to fight on the side of Jordan. Interestingly, as this British threat was delivered British ministers were toying with the idea of pursuing the never-abandoned Anglo-French attack on Egypt, with some kind of Israeli support.

What was going on in the minds of the British cabinet, individually or collectively, at this time, is hard to guage. Eden was

having some difficulty in persuading his colleagues to back him in military action against Egypt. Many, evidently, were concerned about appearances, and there may even have been one or two who objected to the proposed action on moral grounds. Although an invasion of the entire Egyptian territory was not envisaged, the bombing of airfields within range of the Canal Zone and the proposed occupation of the latter was hardly a local police action. It could only be described as an act of war, and civilized society, and especially the English-speaking world,

BELOW: *A gun battery at Ras Nasrani guards the Straits of Tiran, December 1956.*

was expected to begin wars only with a substantial cause at issue, and when there was no prospect of a settlement short of war. What the British cabinet sought was a convincing reason for war, more properly described as a pretext. This was one source of the delay in actually taking action. Another was the obvious desirability of

co-ordinating the proposed operation with Israel whose armed forces, it was realized, were far more formidable than a list of their weapons might have suggested. But evidently the British ministers were determined that there should be no obvious trace of collusion with Israel. The most charitable explanation of this obsession

with appearing whiter than white is that collusion with Israel would have been seen by Britain's diminishing number of friends in the Arab countries as a final and unforgivable betrayal.

In a succession of meetings with the French, the British government evolved a concept which seemed to satisfy all its

supposed needs. For some time, British contact with Israel was through the French, so that it was only rarely and when joint action had already been almost agreed, that British delegates actually entered rooms in which Israelis were present. What the British wanted, and what in essence they finally got, was to

BELOW: *Israeli tank crews replenish their Sherman tanks' ammunition stocks during a lull in the fighting of the Sinai campaign.*

persuade the Israelis to actually start the war, so that the Anglo-French forces could invade the Canal Zone in the guise of peacemakers. When this was first proposed at a meeting in Paris, with a new Israeli delegation which included Ben-Gurion, the latter was initially unwilling to accept such a division of responsibilities; according to Dayan, he said it meant that '. . . Israel volunteered to mount the rostrum of shame so that Britain and France could lave their hands in the waters of purity.'

Dayan, however, considered that the question of purity and impurity concerned the French and British only. It was not Israel which required a pretext, for Nasser had already by his actions provided several. If Britain and France wished to use Israel in this way it did not reflect on Israel, but only on themselves. Israel could regard this accidental ability to provide a pretext simply as an extra bargaining chip to obtain a Franco-British attack on Egypt at the same time as her own. As a meeting attended by Selwyn Lloyd, the British Foreign Secretary, as well as the Israeli and French representatives, Dayan agreed with Ben-Gurion that Israel would not start a war as suggested by the British, but it might start something less than a war. After all, it had a right to

make reprisal raids against the Egyptians in Sinai. The remainder of the discussion revolved largely around a series of bargaining positions in which the precise size and nature of the Israeli attack was debated. The Israelis (Ben-Gurion was now acquiescent) were willing to initiate the whole sequence, but not by launching anything which might be described as a full-scale war. The British were insistent that the Israeli action should be sufficiently large to provide an excuse for the Anglo-French forces to invade in order to prevent the Suez Canal and its traffic being harmed by the fighting.

In the evening of 24 October, two days after this round of talks began, agreement was finally reached and a plan adopted by all three parties. This specified that on 29 October Israel would begin a 'large-scale attack' on Egyptian forces in Sinai, which would be pushed forward the next day to the Suez Canal. On that second day of the plan, the French and British governments would 'appeal' to the government of Egypt to cease fire and withdraw its troops 10 miles from the Canal and accept the entry of Anglo-French troops into the Canal Zone. These troops would secure freedom of traffic along the Canal until a permanent settlement could be

ABOVE: *An Israeli reconnaissance patrol operates in Sinai, October 1956.*
RIGHT: *A captured Egyptian soldier awaits interrogation by the Israelis.*

reached. A simultaneous appeal to Israel would ask for a ceasefire and withdrawal of forces to 10 miles east of the Canal. It would be stated that if one or other of the two governments refused to comply, the Anglo-French forces would use force against them. However, the plan stipulated that if Egypt refused to comply, Israel would not be obliged to cease fire. The expected Egyptian refusal to comply would be followed by an Anglo-French attack on Egyptian forces on 31 October. Israel would send forces to the western shore of the Gulf of Aqaba in order to raise the blockade of Eilat, but undertook not to attack Jordan, in return for which the British government promised not to aid Jordan should the latter attack Israel.

With agreement reached only one week before the Anglo-French forces were to begin hostilities, Israel's preparations needed to be swift. Even before saying goodbye to the French and British representatives, Dayan sent a telegram to his Chief of Operations, ordering immediate mobilization and deceptive measures to give the impression that a substantial action against Jordan was impending. As for the French and the British, their preparations had been proceeding for weeks already, but whether they were far enough advanced to permit the D-Day style of landing envisaged by the British seemed doubtful.

Sinai, which was Israel's chosen and almost inevitable field of battle, is best described as a huge inverted triangle, part of the Middle East but separating it from Africa. Its western side is the longest, being about 310 miles, for the most part along the Gulf of Suez and the Canal. Its northern side is washed by the Mediterranean and is about 135 miles while its eastern side, skirting the Gulf of Aqaba, is about 155 miles. Its southern half is inhospitable and unappealing; sandy and quite mountainous, with no water or greenery. The Egyptians had built a road from Suez along the Gulf of Suez to Sharm el-Sheikh and this was the only reasonable road in the south. The northern half was unpleasant, if a little more welcoming than the southern half. There were a few more roads, mainly built by the Egyptians after the accession of Nasser, to supply new army camps and airfields. Some of the roads had been there in some form for centuries, but had been improved

by the Egyptians. Among these were several east-west links to the Suez canal and some north-south lateral connections between them. The territory in this northern half included scattered oases and their associated villages, but population was generally scanty except along the northern coast. In the center of this northern half was a hilly area, through which the roads ran by means of long and often deep passes.

In October 1956 Nasser was deploying additional troops in Sinai, presumably as part of his intended and preannounced attack on Israel. However, the possibility of some kind of Anglo-French attack following his nationalization of the Canal meant that he had to maintain strong forces to defend the Canal Zone. When the 1956 war started, the Egyptians had two infantry divisions in Sinai. One of these was a Palestinian division, and was based in the Gaza Strip, while the other was deployed around El Arish and Abu Ageila. Smaller formations contrived to cover the rest of the territory. There was an armored brigade which patrolled the area between Bir Gafgafa and Bir El-Hama, and there was an infantry brigade covering the town of Suez just west of the Mitla Pass. There was also a mobile frontier force to patrol the expanses of southern and central Sinai.

The Israeli action that had been the subject of so much bargaining with the British took the form of a paratroop excursion to the eastern end of the Mitla Pass. This was preceded by a sally of Israel's veteran piston-engined Mustang fighters to cut the telephone wires linking Egyptian headquarters and units. For the Mitla drop, which because it was so successful seemed less daring than it really was, the 395-strong 202 Parachute Brigade commanded by Rafael Eitan was carried by 16 Dakotas, 10 Meteor fighters having been scraped together to escort them. Further air cover for this vulnerable and vital flight was provided by a dozen Mystère fighters patrolling along the Suez Canal.

This grasp of the eastern end of the Mitla Pass, which was, as had been hoped, unopposed, satisfied all the essential requirements for this initial action. It was close enough to the Canal to appear to threaten the safe operation of that waterway, but it was not so big as to cause the Egyptians to think that it was anything more than a rather substantial reprisal raid; a subsequent drop of four 106mm antitank guns and a couple of heavy mortars might have caused the Egyptians to doubt their initial appreciation, had they known of it. When the second phase

of this initial operation began, the securing of road access to the Mitla Pass bridgehead, it seemed to the Egyptians that a retreat road for the paratroopers was being established, whereas it was a supply route that was being won. This overland advance was undertaken by the remainder of the 202 Parachute Brigade. Commanded by Arik Sharon, these men had initially been concentrated, for deception purposes, close to the Jordanian frontier but, just as the paratroopers were hurling themselves out of their Dakotas over Mitla, Sharon's men, having marched 65 miles already across the Negev, crossed into Sinai. They were organized into two battalions of parachute troops, a couple of battalions in half-track carriers, a battalion of heavy mortars, an artillery battalion with British 25-pounders, and a tank company with just 13 AMX light tanks. The first serious obstacle to the advance of Sharon's paratroopers was the town of Kuntilla, close inside the frontier and defended by a platoon of Egyptian infantry. This platoon, however, was soon put to flight by the Israeli reconnaissance unit which was preceding the main body; by moving so as to attack from the west this unit confused the defenders and gained the advantage of advancing with the sun behind it. More serious was the resistance expected at the

next settlement along the road, Themed. Here the Egyptians were protected by minefields and barbed wire, and were in greater strength. The road here was bordered by ridges, in which the defenders' machine guns and artillery had been emplaced. By this time, because of the difficult sand-encumbered route, Sharon had lost the use of many vehicles, and to the difficulties caused by breakdowns had been added a fuel shortage which threatened to curtail the use of his remaining vehicles; at this stage he had only two serviceable tanks left. However, the latter were put to good use in strengthening the Israeli assault, which was made with the aid of half-track infantry carriers and jeeps. Within an hour, confused by the dust and smoke raised by the Israeli vehicles, which again had been deployed so as to attack with the sun behind them, the two Egyptian defending companies of infantry were shattered. The final defended locality, rather more than halfway toward Mitla, was Nakhle. Resistance here should have been stiff, for not only was it the base of a battalion of the Egyptian frontier force, but also a training area for *Fedayeen*. But although there was a short air attack on the paratroopers by Egyptian MiG and Vampire jet aircraft, the local defenders were

easily overcome by an artillery bombardment. A few hours later, having cleared the road from Israel to Mitla, Sharon's men joined their comrades who had been dropped at Mitla the previous night.

By this time, the evening of 30 October, the Egyptian command was just beginning to realize that if this was an Israeli retributive raid it was being conducted on a scale hitherto unknown. Apart from the Mitla operation, Israeli troops were now in action in the Abu Ageila area. That morning the Egyptian Minister of Defense (who was also the C-in-C), Abd el Hakim Amer, decided to return to Egypt, cutting short a visit he was making to Jordan. That visit had been to arrange final details of the coordination of the Jordanian army with those of Egypt and Syria, following Jordan's agreement to the principle of a joint command (which had the effect of putting the Jordanian Army under an Egyptian operational commander). Even before Amer's return, some troop movements had been ordered. In particular the 2nd Brigade moved from Suez toward Mitla and one of its battalions, despite losses inflicted by Israeli air attacks, reached the western end of the Mitla Pass where,

BELOW: *The Egyptian destroyer* Ibrahim el Awal *surrendered to the Israeli navy.*

ABOVE: *British-supplied 25-pounders abandoned by the Egyptians at Abu Ageila in the Sinai.*
RIGHT: *A captured Egyptian NCO.*

hidden in the deep rocky ridges and caves, it was safe from air attack.

Meanwhile, the Egyptian Navy was ordered to make its own retributive strike, and this took the form of sending the destroyer *Ibrahim el Awal* (formerly the British *Mendip*) to bombard Haifa. The vessel carried out this order, but was then pursued by Israeli warships and aircraft. Having lost the use of their rudder and part of their electrical system, the Egyptian officers decided that the most promising course of action would be a surrender. They hauled down their flag and were boarded by the Israeli sailors on 31 October. The *Ibrahim el Awal*, renamed *Haifa*, later served in the Israeli Navy.

The operations around Abu Ageila were aimed at the Egyptian fortified zone that had been constructed there, and consisted of a number of strongpoints arranged for mutual support, rather like the German defensive 'hedgehogs' of World War II. As an important part of the Israeli war aims was the shattering of the Egyptian armed forces, the circumstance that a sizable part of the Egyptian Army was located in this area made it an important objective. Moreover, this defense complex commanded the east-west road from the Israeli frontier across the central part of northern Sinai to the Canal at Ismailia.

Free use of this road was essential for the later stages of the Israeli plan of operations. Three Israeli brigades (the 4th and 10th infantry, and the 7th Armored) were entrusted with this series of battles, which continued from 29 October to 2 November, with each strongpoint being successively overcome.

First to fall was Kusseima, an outpost near the frontier held by little more than two battalions of Egyptian frontier guards. At first Israeli progress was slow, hindered more by the terrain than by Egyptian resistance. As this early stage was vital, an earlier-than-planned deployment of the 7th Armored Brigade was made which, in the event, was unnecessary because the infantry captured the Egyptian position before the arrival of the tanks. However, the early availability of these tanks enabled a change of plan to be made. A mixed force under Avraham Adan, then a lieutenant colonel, was sent along the road toward Abu Ageila to reconnoiter the Egyptian defenses to the south of that strongpoint. It was found that the Egyptian deployment of guns in this sector, and especially of the self-propelled British-built Archer antitank guns, was too formidable an obstacle to an assault by the relatively small Israeli armored force. Adan then dispatched most of his force further west, where it was discovered that the Daika Pass, although only fit for tracked vehicles, would permit an assault on Abu

Ageila from the west.

Abu Ageila was well-prepared for an attack, with well-developed minefields, barbed wire obstacles, and preranged artillery which consisted of almost 50 25-pounders and Archers. Artillery support could also be obtained from nearby strongpoints, and notably from the Rueffa Dam. But Abu Ageila did fall quite quickly to an Israeli attack from the west by Adan's armor and motorized infantry. However, Adan's men continued to suffer from gunfire directed from nearby Egyptian strongpoints, and the Israeli force that had been reserved for the reduction of the Rueffa Dam strongpoint had to be diverted to block the road from Ismailia, along which a strong Egyptian armored force, the 1st Armored Brigade, was said to be advancing to the relief of the 'hedgehog.' Although this force was soon routed by Israeli aircraft, the armor sent to deal with it did not return but pursued the Egyptian remnants all the way back to the Canal. Eventually, in the evening of 31 October, the same force that had taken Abu Ageila moved on to the Rueffa position. After sustaining much damage from 25-pounder and Archer fire, and having exhausted the ammunition of their main guns, the Israeli tanks, supported by motorized infantry in half-tracks, subdued the staunch Egyptian defenders.

This left a small area around the strongpoints of Um-Katel and Um-Shihan to

ABOVE: *A reconnaissance patrol keeps watch in the Sinai, November 1956.*

be captured. The initial Israeli attacks were unsuccessful, and Dayan ascribed this to the lack of enthusiasm shown by the 10th Brigade, which was a reserve infantry unit. In this belief he had the 10th Brigade commander replaced. In retrospect, however, it seems that this was an unjustified aspersion. The unit in question had not been trained to attack this kind of objective and moreover was not properly equipped nor provided with adequate intelligence. When the experienced 37th Armored Brigade was sent to help it was no more successful, and suffered severe casualties. Eventually, the positions were won only because the defenders, believing they might be cut off, slipped quietly away, unmolested.

While the battle for Abu Ageila was raging, the paratroopers of General Sharon were in serious trouble at the Mitla Pass. 'Arik' Sharon is frequently described as a 'swashbuckler,' although his enemies have used harsher terms. In the Mitla Pass events he appears to have displayed that brand of unscrupulous cunning of which his critics often complained. Taking advantage of the battle-winning informality of the Israeli forces, which encouraged commanders to go beyond their orders if in their judgment it was advantageous to do so, Sharon appears to have deceived

ABOVE: *Israeli troops advance through typical desert terrain in the Sinai.*
LEFT: *A T-34 is hit by Israeli shellfire.*

his superiors and thereby in addition to sacrificing his men to no good purpose also incurred the displeasure of, among others, Dayan. Sharon, aware that Egyptian forces were installing themselves in the western part of the Mitla Pass, thought it would be a good idea if his troops cleared the entire Pass; the existing Israeli position at the east end was not easily defended in any case and there seemed little point in holding one end of a pass that could not be used for passage. In fact, the possession of the Mitla Pass was of little use to the Israelis, whose plan of operations did not require an open route at that place. As has been explained, the Mitla Pass had been made an Israeli objective specifically because it met the British need for a substantial threat to the Suez Canal, thereby providing a pretext for Anglo-French intervention. Therefore, when Sharon asked permission to clear the Pass, Dayan replied that he could advance, but only at patrol strength. Sharon thereupon organized a 'patrol' consisting of two infantry companies accompanied by tanks and field guns. This was a clear subterfuge which might have been forgiven a Suvorov or a Nelson, and might have been forgiven Sharon, too, had he been successful. But he was not. Soon after entering the narrow pass, Sharon's so-called patrol found itself under fire from Egyptians ensconced on its high sides. Losses were heavy, especially when the Egyptian Air Force joined in. Eventually, after an afternoon of ill-fated fighting, Sharon sent an infantry battalion to help. This climbed the steep sides of the Pass, taking one Egyptian position after another, but only at the expense of heavy losses. In the end the Egyptian losses exceeded the Israeli in this battle (there were about 160 casualties among Sharon's men), and the Egyptians retreated back to the Canal. But the operation, though it could be dressed up to look like a success, was in reality an unnecessary and costly endeavor. Sharon was severely reprimanded by Dayan, but the latter was subsequently criticized for not having dismissed him. In this operation Sharon, despite his intuitive competence and bravery, confirmed the distrust with which he was regarded by many of his fellow officers, a distrust which made it seem unlikely that he would ever rise to the top of the army. In fact, by a subsequent shift from a

military to a political career he would rise even higher than the army, becoming Minister of Defense in 1981.

The capture of the Abu Ageila 'hedgehog' placed the Israeli forces in a good position to either attack or cut off the strong Egyptian formations in the Gaza Strip and just outside the Gaza Strip, at Rafah. Rafah had once been a British army camp and was a military settlement that had been fortified by the Egyptians. It was entrusted to the Egyptian Army's 6th Infantry Brigade, supported by artillery and tank units and by the dedicated if ill-disciplined volunteers of the 87th Palestinian Brigade. To master these defenses the Israeli command allocated two brigades, the 1st Infantry and the 27th Armored. The latter was commanded by Chaim Bar-Lev, a Yugoslav who had already distinguished himself in 1948 and was destined to rise high in the IDF. His brigade consisted of a motorized infantry battalion with Super-Sherman, Sherman and AMX tanks. The Israeli plan was for two infantry battalions to cross from Israel and clear a way through the mine-

fields blocking that line of approach. This would enable armor and further infantry to pass through in preparation for a north-ward movement against the strong defenses located around the Rafah road junction. Meantime two other infantry battalions were to take the defended hills overlooking the Rafah-Gaza road. Part of the Armored Brigade was to cross from Israeli territory into the camp area and drive through the complex while other tanks were to support the various infantry advances. Initially this operation went well, the leading battalion finding its way through the mine-field without difficulty. But when further units came the same way, they ran into mines, losing men, vehicles, and two Super-Sherman tanks. All this commotion attracted strong Egyptian fire, so the several hours spent by the remaining units traversing this route were costly. However,

RIGHT: *Israeli troops overrun a machine-gun position at Rafah, 1 November 1956.*
BELOW: *An Israeli Sherman advances on Rafah, which was strongly held by the Egyptians.*

ABOVE: *An infantry patrol moves toward Rafah on the night of 31 October 1956. By dawn the next day the position had fallen.*

LEFT: *The spoils of war at Rafah included this portrait of President Nasser.*

in the end they got through and successfully assaulted the road junction. The other two infantry battalions, after experiencing initial difficulty in penetrating the wire obstacles under heavy fire, similarly fulfilled their plan. The main force of the Armored Brigade, consisting of motorized infantry with AMX light tanks in support, encountered strong defensive positions which included 17 Archers. The Archers were destroyed by the infantry who, after bitter fighting, reached positions from which they could open fire on the Archers with bazookas. By dawn on 1 December the various Israeli units, having overrun Rafah, linked up again amid self-congratulatory rejoicing and set out westward toward the town of El Arish. A full-scale assault on this town proved unnecessary. Its defenders, like other Egyptian units in Sinai, had been ordered to cross to the western shore of the Canal in order to strengthen the forces already in place; the Egyptian command was readying itself to receive the expected Anglo-French invasion.

By this stage the Israeli forces, despite having routed much of the Egyptian Army, had lost only about 100 men killed. Egyptian losses were considerably greater, although not revealed. In prisoners alone the Egyptians had lost several thousand soldiers, even though the Israeli operations had not been designed to envelop opposing units. In fact, the Israeli command preferred to put the Egyptian troops to flight, because prisoners were a nuisance in a fast-moving campaign. More in conformity with Israeli intentions were the abandoned guns, tanks and vehicles which now littered the routes through Sinai, victims of Israeli air strikes or of breakdowns and fuel shortages while in retreat. The destruction of Egypt's war potential had been a prime aim of the Israeli campaign, and these remnants demonstrated that the object had been largely achieved. So numerous were the items abandoned by the Egyptians that it was soon found worthwhile to add several varieties of captured weapon to the Israeli arsenal as

standard items, using the damaged units to provide spare parts. In this way much Soviet equipment, including tanks, was acquired by the IDF. Ex-British items, like the veteran 25-pounder gun, could be absorbed by the Israeli Army without any need for retraining or any problems concerning ammunition supply.

The air war, however, had not produced such favorable results for the Israelis. Because this was a war which in some respects had deliberately been launched at half-cock, Israeli aircraft had hardly touched Egyptian airfields. Most air engagements took place over Sinai in the first couple of days, before the Egyptians began to withdraw their air force to meet an anticipated Anglo-French onslaught. In these encounters the Israeli Mystères proved superior to the Egyptian MiG aircraft, and about five MiGs were destroyed, as well as older types. The two Israeli Mystères lost seem to have been victims of ground fire, as were the nine losses of older types. These numbers, while increasing the self-confidence of the Israeli Air Force, did little to reduce the disparity in numbers; the Egyptian Air Force continued to be about one-and-a-half times larger than the Israeli. However, this disparity would be reversed when the British and French air forces intervened.

The Israeli victories at Rafah and the dissolution of the Egyptian headquarters organization at El Arish meant that the 10,000 or so Egyptian and Palestinian troops in the Gaza Strip were in a difficult position, despite their possession of more than a dozen fortified areas within that territory. As usual, the Israeli force sent to capture the Strip relied on an assault force composed of Sherman tanks and half-track infantry carriers. This force was sent in against the opposing line behind an artillery barrage. An assault such as this penetrated the outer and key defenses of Gaza and led to an Egyptian

BELOW: *Infantry advance on Rafah.*
BOTTOM: *A captured Egyptian antitank gun position is camouflaged with netting.*

surrender of the city. The surrender not only preserved many Egyptian lives, but also saved the Israelis possible trouble from the 200,000 Palestinian refugees festering on the outskirts of the city. Elsewhere in the Strip, fighting lasted longest around Khan Yunis. The defenders here, as in much of the Strip, were Palestinians, and fought staunchly.

Although at this time the Anglo-French armed intervention was getting under way, the Israeli government rightly surmised that sooner or later the great powers, or more probably the United Nations, would impose a ceasefire. Before this happened, it was considered essential to achieve a main object of the campaign, the expulsion of the Egyptians from Sharm El-Sheikh which would lift the blockade of Eilat. A preliminary move toward this end had been made on the first day of the war, when a small force left Eilat and seized the nearby road junction of Ras el-Naqb. As in 1948 and in subsequent wars, roads and road junctions were key objectives in this campaign. This particular move assured free passage to Eilat from the Kuntilla direction and, more important, opened the way for a move down the eastern coast of Sinai to the final objective of Sharm El-Sheikh. The east coast road, about 150 miles long, was in reality little more than an upgraded camel track which

TOP LEFT: *An Israeli patrol moves through the streets of newly captured El Arish.*
LEFT: *A position at Sharm-el-Sheikh.*
BELOW: *Women of the IDF Signals Corps.*

ABOVE: *Prisoners at Sharm-el-Sheikh.*
LEFT: *Moshe Dayan confers with the Air Force commander, Dan Tolkovsky (beret).*

rose up jagged mountain sides and descended into ravines and sandy valleys, all in conditions of dry heat, total absence of water and almost total absence of vegetation. The 9th Infantry Brigade, which was ordered to proceed down this road, was a reserve unit commanded by Avraham Yoffe, a former officer of the British Army. It started off with 200 vehicles and 1800 men and, to its credit arrived, a week after setting out from Kuntilla, with almost the same strength. It had been arranged that tanks would be shipped by the Israeli Navy from Eilat and handed over to the 9th Infantry in time for the attack on Ras Nasrani, a defended outpost just north of Sharm El-Sheikh. Other landing craft had been allocated to supply the Brigade with fuel and food at points along its route.

Meanwhile a battalion of Sharon's paratroopers had been dispatched south from Mitla along the easier west coast road, preceded by a paratroop drop at El-Tur to secure the airfield and enable an additional infantry battalion to be landed. The general plan was that the Sharm El-Sheikh fortified zone would be assaulted from the east by the 9th Brigade, and from the west by this mixed paratroop and infantry force. As things turned out, it was the 9th Brigade which carried out the Israeli attack, the other force playing a relatively minor role. The attackers enjoyed the advantage of air superiority, for the Egyptian Air Force had no aircraft to spare for this theater. However, the Sharm El-Sheikh fortifications, built with generous use of concrete on high stony ridges, were formidable enough. The first assault, by one of the 9th Brigade's battalions, failed when it ran into minefields and came under artillery fire. An attack by a second battalion, preceded by air and mortar bombardment, was more successful, and Sharm El-Sheikh was in Israeli hands early on 5 November, the day before the UN ceasefire came into force. Israel, it seemed, had managed to attain its war objectives just in time.

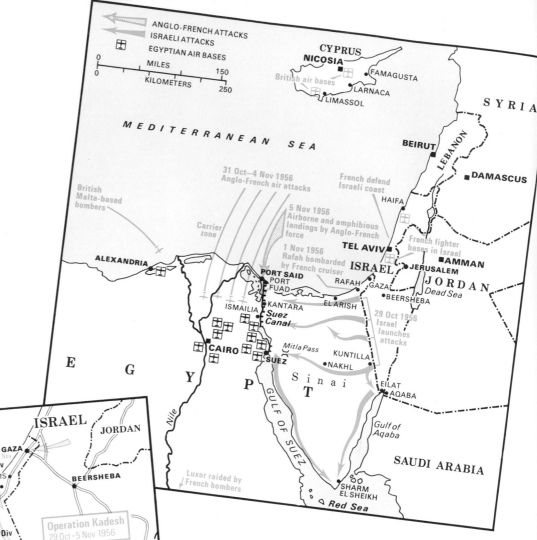

Meanwhile, in what was portrayed by both the Anglo-French and Israeli publicists as a completely different operation, the French and British were organizing their own campaign against Nasser. The first element of the plan, well concealed until it actually occurred, was the fulfilment of Britain's undertaking to Israel to destroy the Egyptian bomber force. The Israeli government had agreed to start the war, in the unusual way already described, only on condition that Israeli cities would be protected from Egyptian bombing. This meant that the British were required to attack the Egyptian airfields as soon as, or before, the Egyptian government concluded that the Israeli activity in Sinai was something more than a small-scale operation. With her airfields in Cyprus, Britain was well-placed to undertake this task. It began on the night of 31 October with attacks on the Kabrit, Inchass, Almaza and Abu Suweir airfields, followed by five more targets the next morning. Technically, these attacks were a masterpiece, with bombing so accurate that Egypt's bomber force was destroyed, without any accidental damage to civilian objects. Apart from destroying Nasser's twin-engined bombers, other aircraft were hit too, making effective Egyptian ground-attack operations in the subsequent days a rarity.

RIGHT: *Israeli infantry men in their trench.*
LEFT AND ABOVE: *Maps illustrate the 1956 war.*

Because the British had set their hearts on a grand invasion, founded on the Normandy experience of 1944, the Anglo-French planning and preparation had not been rapid. Also, because there were no deepwater ports in Cyprus, faraway Malta had to be the base of the naval operation. Under General Keightley, Lieutenant General Stockwell (encountered earlier in the Haifa evacuation of 1948) was in charge of the Anglo-French land forces. Both Keightley and Stockwell unsuccessfully urged their government to schedule the landing for 1 November, as originally envisaged, rather than 6 November. They were probably right in this, for international pressure was soon applied to the British and in the event the operation had only just begun when the order came for its termination.

RIGHT: *British paratroopers check their equipment before the assault on Suez.*
BOTTOM: *Paratroopers land on El Gamil.*
BELOW: *Supply containers drop from an RAF Hastings over El Gamil airfield.*

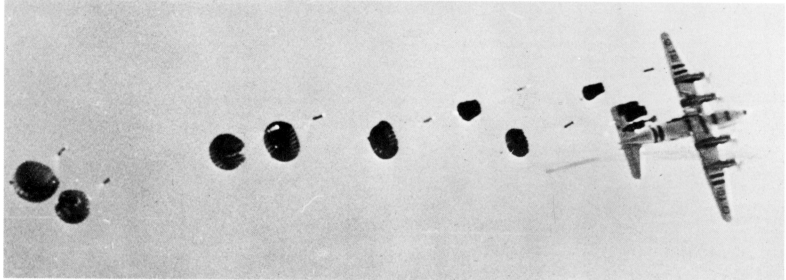

The core of the Anglo-French invasion fleet were British and French aircraft carriers, including the British *Eagle* and *Bulwark*. The British had assembled an infantry division, with a paratroop brigade group and a Commando brigade in support, while the French furnished a paratroop division, plus a paratroop battalion and a light mechanized regiment. The fundamental problem was that this strong army, which had been proclaimed to be a peacekeeping force designed to prevent the Egyptians and Israelis engaging in full-scale battles in the area of the Suez Canal, was scheduled to arrive off the Canal on 6 November. By that time it seemed increasingly likely that the Egyptian-Israeli fighting would have finished anyway; the Israelis had almost reached their alloted positions 10 miles from the Canal, while the Egyptian forces were retreating to the west bank of the Canal. Meanwhile it was only by using the veto (for the first time)

ABOVE: *French troops advance to occupy Port Fouad on 5 November 1956.*
LEFT: *Salvage ships clear Suez harbor.*
BELOW LEFT: *An LST unloads a Centurion tank at Suez.*

that Britain and France were able to squash a proposal in the UN Security Council inviting them to desist. When the debate was transferred to the General Assembly, Britain and France were overwhelmingly outvoted. Only Australia and New Zealand, out of traditional loyalty to London and with uneasy consciences, voted in support of Israel, Britain and France.

Because of these pressures the Anglo-French forces landed a day early; British paratroops dropped at Port Said and French at Port Fouad on 5 November. The next day the main force made beach landings at these points. Although, at the time and later, some Israelis poked fun at the somewhat cumbersome British planning process, in fact the planning had produced good results, with the landings accomplished with scant loss. For the first time in warfare, helicopters played a leading part in moving the invading troops, and this ability to transfer men swiftly and unexpectedly was one of the factors responsible for the low casualties. It was intended to advance from Port Said southward, capturing Ismailia on 8 November and Suez on 12 November.

On 6 November the Egyptian commander at Port Said agreed to discuss terms for a surrender of the city and then decided he could not accept the terms offered. In the meantime, as had been feared by the British government, fighting between Israelis and Egyptians had already petered out on 4 November. At this point, with their original pretext for the landings looking even more tattered, British ministers began to talk of a Russian plot to take over the Middle East that they had fore-

ABOVE: *The Suez Canal at Port Said was closed by Egyptian blockships.*
LEFT: *Royal Marine Commandos raise the White Ensign over Navy House, Port Said.*

stalled. In an effort at least to achieve something before the inevitable imposition of a ceasefire, the British commander prepared to send his troops south by helicopter, by-passing Port Said, where fierce fighting still continued. However, before this advance could be properly launched the British government finally agreed to a ceasefire at midnight on 6/7 November.

Although it was possible for powers like Britain and France to defy the UN, although at the price of their hitherto respected reputations, pressure from the USA, though quiet, had proved irresistible. The Anglo-French forces had not succeeded in preventing the Egyptians sinking blockships in the Canal which,

among other things, interrupted oil shipments. Additionally, oil pipelines passing through Syria to the Mediterranean had been sabotaged, and Saudi Arabia embargoed oil shipments to France and Britain in protest at their actions. This meant that Britain would have to obtain her oil from dollar suppliers. In anticipation of this, and of the damage the hostilities were expected to inflict on the British economy, the pound fell. Soon the only solution seemed to be the purchase of oil and other essential imports by means of an American credit. But Washington, feeling deceived by Paris and London, was in no mood to be co-operative, and it was the need to satisfy US demands that eventually forced London to agree to evacuate the troops.

Although US pressure was decisive, the British government had also been weakened in its resolve by the disapproval

of Commonwealth governments, and by a split in British public opinion. Although it was only after petrol rationing was imposed in Britain that the Conservative government began to alarm its own supporters, the earlier failure to secure all-party support for the Suez venture, and to secure media support for the government, seriously weakened the British action. In this campaign the British and French armed forces performed very well, but were ill-served by their respective governments.

When the British agreed to a ceasefire the French had little option but to follow suit; the circumstance that the two nation's forces were operating under joint command was enough to make it impossible for the French to pursue the campaign without the British. Thus the war ended in early November, although it was not until March 1957, when the Israelis

ABOVE: *The debris of war in the Sinai included this burned-out T-34 tank.*
TOP LEFT: *Moshe Dayan (front right) confers with United Nations observers, 1956.*
LEFT: *Israeli artillery pictured during the withdrawal from the Sinai.*

marched out of the Gaza Strip, that the postwar settlement came into force.

This settlement had been arranged in the United Nations, where Israel, France and Britain were in various degrees of disfavor among the representatives of the member nations. In these circumstances, the agreements reached were not as ungenerous as the Israelis liked to claim even though, as time would show, the international guarantees which formed part of this settlement were not as irrevocable as Israel needed for an assurance of a peaceful, unthreatened, future. Israel, even more than Britain, was highly dependent on American goodwill, as it received much financial aid from America. It was therefore in no condition to resist American pressure designed to persuade it to withdraw from Sharm El-Sheikh, the main Israeli gain of the war. However, to help persuade the reluctant Israeli government, it was arranged that this key position would not be controlled by Egyptian forces but would (like the Gaza Strip) be rendered innocuous by the stationing of an international peacekeeping force under UN auspices. For 10 years this arrangement proved successful, to the benefit of Eilat and the Israeli economy. In Gaza the outcome was less satisfactory for Israel, for the UN forces there had to coexist with an Egyptian military governor, and to some extent the Strip continued to be used as a base for *Fedayeen* raids into Israel.

BELOW: *American Marines from the US Sixth Fleet land at Beirut, 18 July 1958.*

REGROUPING AND REARMAMENT

Having got the better of two big powers, France and Britain, Nasser's prestige was considerably enhanced by the 1956 war. The defeat of the Egyptian forces by the Israelis was obscured or, at worst, passed off as a consequence of Egypt's need to defend herself on two fronts. It seems that what was initially a purely propaganda device became, as often happens, a belief, with the result that the fundamental weaknesses of the Egyptian forces in relation to Israel were never rigorously analyzed. In any case, it was supposed that in a future war Egypt would receive more armed help from Israel's other Arab neighbors; in 1956, Egypt had fought alone, much to the disgust of its people.

If the Egyptians had engaged in a critical study of their own and Israel's forces, they might have discovered certain essential truths which, in the wars of 1967 and 1973, would again result in a poor showing of their forces. A basic problem was that Egypt was socially and economically undeveloped. This meant that her population had not yet acquired the skills and the attitudes which are needed if young men are to make good twentieth-century soldiers. A population whose mental and physical rhythms are conditioned by the seasons and the time of day is unlikely to produce soldiers of great energy, endurance, and alertness. A population which has little experience of using machinery is not likely to produce enough young men to handle tanks, artillery and radar effectively. True, given sufficient training, the Egyptian young man was quite capable of mastering technique, but for an army of short-term conscripts this was a serious problem. Secondly, economic backwardness meant that other countries had to be relied on for the supply of arms. Israel had the same problem, and both countries found that dependence on foreign suppliers influenced their foreign and military policies, the supplying countries being able to threaten a cessation of supplies as the ultimate means of persuasion. Moreover, acceptance of arms from just one country (which was usually advantageous, for reasons of standardization), meant that military doctrine, training and tactics began to follow the pattern of the supplying country's forces; the influx of foreign specialists to assist in training was a strong impulse in this process. For Egypt, this circumstance was highly disturbing. Most of her officers had been brought up according to British Army practices and traditions, and a high proportion, especially among the most successful officers, was British-trained. After 1955 the substitution of British practices by Soviet, with Egyptian officers going to Russia for training and others being trained at home by Russians, induced a kind of schizophrenia in the Egyptian forces. Whereas Israeli commanders might have differences of

ABOVE: *Egyptian refugees return to El Arish, following the Israeli withdrawal under United Nations supervision in 1957.*
TOP: *Yugoslavian troops of the United Nations peacekeeping forces in the Sinai are interviewed by journalists in January 1957.*

opinion which sometimes might be long lasting, Egyptian commanders suffered from much more acute differences, differences of military philosophy. To this it might be added that neither British or Russian military doctrine and practice was really suited to Egyptian circumstances. The British and the Russians were trained to fight large-scale wars, where faultless organization of numerous and complex formations was required. The

Middle East wars in which Egypt engaged were small both in numbers involved and in distances. It is noteworthy that in the 1956 war the Israeli formations were no larger than brigades. Israeli operating formations of division strength simply did not exist, and this continued to be the case.

Largely because of the way the Israeli forces had grown and developed since the 1940s, they had their own unique style and philosophy. One key advantage was their reserve and mobilization system, which benefited from a population which had no differences about the goal (which was survival) and which by and large was sufficiently educated and disciplined to produce good soldiers without long periods

fixed fortifications after 1967, they suffered setbacks.

Nasser's basic error, in his wars of 1956 and 1967, was to provoke hostilities before the long-term weaknesses of the Egyptian state and its army had been corrected. Whether his was the impatience of a man in search of greatness and of popular applause, or of a man burning to right wrongs and erase shame, is immaterial. Egypt, and the Arabs in general, needed a preparation time which would have been longer than Nasser's remaining lifespan. It was Nasser's reluctance, or inability, to see this which detracts most from his image as a hero figure; even though he did do his best to remedy Egypt's economic weaknesses (with, notably, the Aswan Dam project), the result of his policies was debilitating because Egypt was in no condition to maintain the military posture he imposed.

Nevertheless, in the period separating the 1956 and 1967 wars Nasser was able to pursue his aims by means other than war. He was wildly popular among Arabs who had long needed a hero figure, especially one who seemed so capable of humiliating the British and French. The influence of Britain and France in the Middle East up to the 1950s had aroused considerable resentment, partly because no nation likes to see foreigners dominating its affairs, partly because many of the defects and wrongs of life in these countries could be ascribed, rightly or wrongly, to the foreigner. In general, the Arabs of the Middle East were right to believe that they had not attained a dignified position in the world, and that such a position was not only their right but within their capabilities. They were usually wrong to imagine that the removal of foreign influence would bring an instant renewal. There was too much wrong with Arab society, which was still feudal or semifeudal in its attitudes (and often in its structure too) with too many beliefs, attitudes, and aspirations which simply did not fit in with the modern world. Repeated defeats inflicted by Israel, beginning with the creation of that state in 1948, only served to turn resentment of the foreigner into hatred, without causing Arabs to look more closely at themselves so as to discover precisely what needed improvement at home. In general, the British and French mistake (repeated subsequently by the Americans) was to lend their support to established rulers, sometimes feudal and tyrannical, and hence to tradition itself. In other words, Western influence tended to delay necessary change, and this is the real criticism that can be leveled at the west.

Throughout the 11 years 1956–67, years of neither peace nor war, Nasser and Nasserism strengthened their hold on the Middle East, and Nasser's anti-Western stand was probably his most potent

of full-time training. The informality of the forces, and the primacy of the small unit in operations, together with the acceptance that the officer on the spot had a right, even a duty, to depart from instructions received from above where circumstances seemed to indicate such a departure, were incalculable advantages. The Israeli command was well aware of the flexibility which this situation created, and the advantage it gave the Israelis over the Egyptians; the latter fought well so long as circumstances conformed to their previously elaborated plans, but when the unexpected happened both the Egyptian officers and their men were slow to regain their composure – often fatally slow. It therefore became a key Israeli technique

ABOVE: *The carrier HMS* Victorious *(foreground) and the commando carrier HMS* Bulwark *supported the British in Kuwait. A Scimitar is landing on* Victorious.
TOP: *In 1961 British forces were sent to Kuwait to prevent its annexation by Iraq. The illustration shows a Bren-gun position.*

to so conduct war as to present the Egyptians with unexpected circumstances right from the start. Once having got the enemy on the run, the Israelis could expect to retain the initiative and thereby more than compensate for their numerical inferiority. It is noteworthy that when the Israelis departed from this approach, for example, by constructing the Bar-Lev Line of weapon in winning the hearts and minds of Arab populations and thereby undermining the existing Arab governments and regimes. Injections of Egyptian money and arms for the benefit of Nasserite factions was also a feature, although this was much exaggerated by Nasser's enemies. The upheavals which took place in several Arab capitals, resulting in the installation of anti-Western governments of a self-proclaimed revolutionary nature, were not explicable solely in terms of Egyptian subversion, as the Western press usually claimed, but certainly owed much to the inspiration provided by Nasser's successful anti-Westernism, and his promise to continue the struggle against Israel, a struggle which other Arab rulers preferred to wage by empty words.

In 1958, the pro-Western Hashemite monarchy was overthrown by a military coup in Iraq. King Feisal and his family were murdered, and his prime minister,

the fairly level-headed Nuri Said, was torn to pieces by a mob after initially going into hiding dressed as an old woman. The army officer Abdul Kassem, of doubtful mental stability, led the new regime which, though claiming to be revolutionary, did not change very much except the country's alliances. British influence there was finally ended, and the USSR became Iraq's patron, much to the alarm of the Western powers (and also of Nasser, who believed that Kassem's persecution of Nasserites was a result of communist influence). At about the same time serious unrest broke out in Lebanon. This state, an artificial creation in which a careful structure kept the Christian and Muslim sections of the population in a state of peaceful and quite prosperous coexistence, was obviously very vulnerable to any outside pressure. This knowledge had been one of the factors which, after 1948, dissuaded it from involving itself in conflict with its southern neighbor, Israel. However, part of the Muslim population was sufficiently inspired by Nasserism to provoke what seemed to be the beginning of a civil war. The Lebanese President, Chamoun, thereupon invited US assistance.

The American Sixth Fleet, cruising in the Mediterranean, was diverted to Beirut, where it landed Marines in sufficient force to save the situation and permit a restoration of the status quo. In Jordan, too, outside intervention saved the regime. There, King Hussein had for some time been the target of vicious attacks by, among other media, Cairo radio, and when he seemed in danger from local revolutionaries the British sent troops by air to the capital, Amman. Both the British and the American interventions were loudly condemned by, among others, Cairo and Moscow. However, they preserved the status quo.

In Syria the pro-Nasser Ba'ath Party gained power and agreed to a 'sacred and indissoluble union' of Syria and Egypt. However, this lasted only until 1961. It entailed the formation of the United Arab Republic, consisting of two 'regions,' Syria and Egypt. Despite protestations about the essential equality of the two partners, Syrians came to see this union as a device for subordinating Damascus to Cairo, an impression which seemed to be confirmed when the Egyptian General Hakim Amer, resident in Syria as Nasser's representative, began to act like a governor-general. Nevertheless, after the split some

TOP: *King Feisal II of Iraq was overthrown in 1958 and he and his family murdered.*
LEFT: *A US Marine M-48 tank in Beirut in support of the Lebanese Government.*
BELOW: *US Marines in Beirut, 1958.*
RIGHT: *Paratroopers board in Cyprus en route to Jordan.*

LEFT: *An Israeli soldier removes the bodies of Syrians killed in a border clash, 1962.*
ABOVE: *In 1958 Britain sent the Red Devils to Jordan in support of King Hussein's regime which was under attack by revolutionaries.*
RIGHT: *Locals watch Red Devils drill with a bazooka at Amman airport, Jordan.*

co-operation continued in anti-Israeli activities.

Syrian access to northern Israel was a great advantage to Nasser, because the existence of the UN Peacekeeping Force in the Gaza strip meant that *Fedayeen* raids from there were hindered, and could not develop into large-scale incursions. Apart from being a good launching site for such raids, Syria could, and did, take advantage of its possession of the Golan Heights to subject Israeli settlements to sporadic artillery fire. It was in response to raids from Syria that in 1960 Israel renewed its old policy of retributive raids. The Syrian intelligence service was invaluable, supplying information not only about Israel, but about Lebanon, Jordan and Iraq as well.

In Jordan various attempts to assassinate King Hussein, still regarded as an enemy by Nasser, were assisted by the Syrians. One plot did succeed in killing Hussein's prime minister, and it appears to have been only British pressure which dissuaded Hussein from launching a war against Syria forthwith. In 1966 Hussein was considerably weakened in popular esteem, and forced to rely more on his Bedouin supporters. After a number of *Fedayeen* raids against Israel had been launched from Jordanian territory, Israel struck back in an unprecedented daylight operation involving tanks and aircraft, destroying a village in the Hebron Hills. A reprisal raid of this size and nature inevitably bore much of the character of an atrocity which the King had been unable to prevent and was unlikely to avenge. To improve the King's prospects of survival,

the USA granted appreciable military aid; Hussein was then at least regarded as a man who could obtain what was needed for an eventual war against Israel.

Israeli hopes that the problem of the Palestinian refugees would one day melt away were again disappointed in 1965, when the Palestine Liberation Organization (PLO) was formally inaugurated at a conference in Jerusalem. The head of this organization was Ahmed Shukeiri, and it was intended to combine, or at least co-ordinate, various factions of the Palestinian movement. Arab states, many of which had ample resources from their oil revenues, provided its funds, and on this basis it began to form a Palestinian Army. Its doctrine was enunciated in the Palestinian Covenant, which included sections calling for the destruction of Israel as a state and the establishment of a Palestinian state. The idea of founding a new Palestinian state in Jordan's West Bank or the Gaza

Strip, a solution increasingly suggested by other countries wishing to ensure some stability in the Middle East, was not entertained. There was some conflict between the PLO aims and the Arab states, for the PLO wished to provoke a state of war between Israel and its Arab neighbors as soon as possible whereas many Arab governments, while accepting this as an objective, somehow thought that the propitious moment was always the day after tomorrow.

Meanwhile, another blow could be struck against Israel by nonmilitary means. To residents of temperate climates, the emotional tension surrounding the supply of water in dry areas of the world is difficult to imagine, but is nevertheless real. In such countries water is seen not only to be the source and supporter of all life, but a commodity which is not inevitably in secure supply. In Israel the influx of immigrants had to some extent been diverted to the countryside, where new

and old agricultural settlements were engaged in making the desert bloom. For such projects to be successful, irrigation schemes had to be executed. Sources of water for such schemes were scarce, so the Jordan River was disproportionately important. Unfortunately for the Israelis, this river, before entering Israel, passes through Lebanon and Syria. Study by Arab experts showed that if two major sources of the Jordan, the River Hazbani in Lebanon and the River Banias in Syria, were diverted to the River Yarmuk in Jordan, Israel might well lose two-thirds of the Jordan waters. Israel was well aware of this danger, and had earlier made it clear that a diversion of the Jordan waters would be regarded as an act of war. Nevertheless her northern neighbors went ahead with canal construction to divert the waters. Israel's first reaction was to shell both the canal works which were close to the frontier and to bomb those which were not. This did persuade the Arab governments that a full-scale war with Israel might ensue and they implicitly withdrew their support from this Syrian venture. The diversion work therefore ceased, and was not renewed, although in principle such a diversion still represents a possible means of damaging Israel.

Although Nasser in these years took care to avoid another war with Israel, he was quite prepared to use his forces elsewhere when the conditions were right. In fact, conditions seldom were right, but in 1962 a coup against the royal rulers of Yemen brought a civil war in which Nasser decided to intervene. The Yemeni royalists had found support from Arab kings in Saudi Arabia and Jordan, and the struggle between the royalists and republicans seemed to symbolize the underlying struggle in which progressive Arab forces, of whom Nasser regarded himself as the inspiration and leader, struggled to overcome the centuries-old forces of backwardness represented by the Arab monarchies. Egypt therefore intervened militarily on a large scale (unlike Jordan and Saudi Arabia, whose participation was largely financial and material). By April 1963 Egypt had about 36,000 troops in Yemen, and its aircraft were wreaking great destruction on Yemeni villages in the royalist-held areas. Although the new, supposedly revolutionary, regime was not popular among Yemenis, overseas aid for the royalists was restricted by outside pressures, particularly from the USA, which at that time was reluctant to cause unnecessary offense to Nasser and the social forces which he represented. As early as December 1962 the USA recognized the Yemeni republican government. However, this did not deter the royalist forces within the country who, forced out of the towns, controlled most of the countryside. They had less than 50 French, British and Belgian mercenaries

to advise them, but despite an increase of the Egyptian forces to about 60,000 men by late 1965 neither the Egyptians nor the Yemeni republicans could dislodge the royalists. Egyptian offensives, planned on a grand scale, came to grief with heavy losses; on one occasion the lightly armed royalists, aided by local mud, knocked out 10 Egyptian tanks. After 1965 the royalists managed to acquire mortars and bazookas and despite their inability to work together pushed the Egyptians and republicans into a small number of towns. Finally, after the 1967 War against Israel, Nasser was so short of money that he agreed to withdraw his support from the Yemeni republicans in return for financial aid from his recent arch-enemy, the King of Saudi Arabia. After this, with the republican leadership trimmed by a series of internal coups, the war petered out in a compromise peace in 1969, just as the royalists, faced by heavy subsidization of the republicans by the USSR, seemed to

LEFT: *A derelict Egyptian T-34/85 tank is inspected by Royalists in Yemen.*
BELOW: *A British 105mm Howitzer in Yemen.*

be facing defeat; a coalition government was formed including both republicans and royalists. This effectively ended the seven-year Yemeni civil war. The cost to Nasser had been high. He had not scored the quick victory he had hoped, his troops had proved ineffective against tribesmen secure in their mountainous countryside, Egypt had spent more money than it could afford, his intervention brought disapproval for different reasons from Arab friends and enemies and also from neutral countries (especially after it was reported that the Egyptians were using poison gas against Yemeni villages). Nasser's inter-

BELOW: *King Hussein met Amer, C-in-C of the joint Arab command, in 1964.*

pursue any policy that might bring on full-scale war in the Middle East. He was aware that Israel was receiving military supplies from Western countries, and for one reason or another usually overestimated the numbers of weapons involved in these transactions. Since he symbolized, and was determined to continue to symbolize, the cause of Arab radicalism and anti-Westernism, he could not hope to purchase arms in France, Britain or the USA and was therefore dependent on the USSR. For its part, the USSR was anxious to increase its influence in the Middle East, largely as a means to weaken the West, and in Nasser it felt it had a potential ally with tolerable philosophies. Perhaps with a touch of wishful thinking, Moscow re-

alysis there was a strong element of muddle which at various junctures would weaken the position of the progressive Arab regimes. For example, the old so-called Western-orientated regimes were just as opposed to Israel as the new regimes (and in the case of Saudi Arabia and the Gulf states, they were in a better position to finance anti-Israeli activity). The treatment of Israel as a US pawn was crucially inaccurate, and hardly conformed to the known facts. The USA in much of this period was steadfastly refusing to supply Israel with weapons; only in the case of Hawk defensive antiaircraft missiles was this attitude relaxed. US financial aid, whose withdrawal would have been catastrophic for Israel, seemed to give the US

vention, however, was supported by the USSR, and the pattern of Soviet arms deliveries was affected by this support. It is unlikely, for example, that the heavy transport aircraft and helicopters supplied by the USSR were intended for use against Israel, but they had an obvious role in Egypt's Yemeni venture.

The size and nature of the Soviet contribution to the Egyptian armed forces was the determining factor in Nasser's foreign policy in this period. So long as the Egyptian President felt that he was militarily inferior to the Israelis, he was unable to

garded Egypt, Iraq, Syria (and later republican Libya) as progressive states which it would be ideologically as well as practically advisable to help in their struggle against both Israel and the remaining traditional Arab regimes. Israel was regarded by Arabs as simply the USA's agent in the Middle East, while the traditional Arab regimes (and Saudi-Arabia was regarded as the most offensive in this respect) were regarded as friends of the West and dependent on Western support for survival amid their hostile local populations. In this ill-formed an-

government great influence in Tel Aviv but Israeli astuteness in utilizing, among other things, the influence of American Jews in American politics and journalism, usually ensured that the USA-Israel relationship was not the normal kind of big power/small power situation.

What Nasser's intentions were in this period of uneasy peace from 1956 to 1967 is unclear, but it may be assumed that at some stage he intended to have another go at Israel; as a military man he felt deeply the Egyptian defeats of 1948 and 1956 and this alone, independently of any feelings

he might have had about the destruction of Israel as a state, would have impelled him to war. Soviet motives in meeting his demands for arms are a little more clear. Moscow intended that Egypt should be strong enough to hold its own against any US-backed Israeli attempt to suppress the 'progressive' regimes in Cairo and Damascus. The Soviet government had persuaded itself that the West would refuse to allow the new Syrian and Egyptian regimes to exist in peace, and would at the right moment take action through Israel. The 1956 war was regarded as confirmation of this view, more attention being paid to the belligerent actions of France and Britain than to the ceasefire that had been imposed, in effect if not blatantly, by the USA. On the other hand,

the prime aim of the Soviet government was to avoid any risk of an armed conflict with the USA, and this not only led to Arab disappointment at the lack of expected Soviet support at critical junctures, but also determined the shape of the Egyptian, Syrian (and to a lesser extent Iraqi) armed forces. These forces were molded by the types of weapons which Russia sent, and Russia was determined not to give these three Arab countries the kinds of weapons with which they might obliterate Israel, for that would provoke a war in which the USA might intervene. Instead the weapons were to be sufficient to deter Israel from aggression and to give the three progressive Arab states the means of backing their diplomacy with the appearance of military power. This is not

ABOVE: *President Nasser (right) confers with the Soviet leaders in Moscow, 1965.*
TOP: *Soviet-supplied SA-2 surface-to-air missiles formed part of the Egyptian air defenses in Sinai in 1967.*

how Russian activity was portrayed in the Western or Israeli press at the time, or indeed later. An oversimple view was presented which, while correctly conveying the Soviet intention to increase its influence in the Middle East, ignored the actual moderation and caution of the Soviet approach. In part, this was a result of the unwillingness, or inability, of the Western media to put perception before dramatization, and in part it was a result of the Israeli success in presenting its struggle for existence as a vital part of that worldwide struggle against communism that had such a wide emotional appeal in the USA.

All the same, Western emphasis on the 'Soviet arms build-up' in the Middle East was neither unsurprising nor inaccurate; in this decade of peace great quantities of weapons were shipped from the USSR to Egypt, Syria and Iraq, which at the time did seem like client states of the USSR. The process began with the Soviet promise to replace the Egyptian losses incurred in the 1956 war, and continued with Soviet-Egyptian arms agreements of 1959, 1961, 1963 and 1965, and subsidiary arrangements with the other two states. It can now be seen that the 1963 and 1965 agreements had the effect of producing the war of 1967, although this was far from the Soviet intention. It is also interesting (and indicative of the strength of the underlying Soviet purpose) that arms deliveries continued even during periods of Soviet-Egyptian coolness, in particular during 1959, when Nasser's persecution of Egyptian communists was arousing Khrushchev's irritation.

With the arms came military advisers from the Soviet Union and from Czechoslovakia. Originally these were intended to provide instruction in the use of the new weapons, but in time they came to influence, if not dictate, the whole military philosophy. From the 1956 war the Soviet Union had drawn an unflattering estimate of Egyptian military competence and it was only natural that Moscow did not wish to see the advantage of Soviet weaponry squandered by what it considered to be outmoded military doctrine and outmoded tactical thought. Hence a creeping Sovietization overtook the forces of Egypt and Syria, and to a lesser extent of Iraq. This was resisted by a sizable proportion of the Egyptian and Syrian officers, who tended to ignore Soviet advice on principle. After the defeats of 1967 the Soviet attitude was that these dissident officers had brought on the catastrophe by doing precisely what they had been advised not to do, and that these men were primarily the older British-influenced officers. In this last assertion the Russians were probably wrong, and their accusation, though not without foundation, is too generalized. The tactical advice given by Soviet advisers to the Egyptian Army was over-rigid, with emphasis on fixed lines of defense which played into the hands of the Israelis' emphasis on the unexpected and the disruptive. However, it seems that this Soviet advice was not given with great conviction. It was simply that the Russian military specialists believed, probably rightly, that the Egyptian Army units at that time were not capable of implementing more refined tactics in the field.

By 1967 the armed forces of Egypt, Syria and Iraq were almost entirely equipped with Soviet weapons, so the replacement of British doctrine and tradition was entirely appropriate. These weapons brought the Middle East conflict to a new stage, both in technology and scale. Egypt, when the war started, possessed 1200 Soviet tanks and self-propelled guns, more than 1500 Soviet guns and mortars, a few odd Soviet missiles for surface-to-surface use, about 500 jet aircraft together with some helicopters and transport aircraft as well as a total of 150 Soviet anti-aircraft missile installations (SAM-2). Soviet equipment supplied to Syria comprised 500 tanks and self-propelled guns, various guns and mortars, 100 jet aircraft, and a dozen SAM-2 installations. Iraq

had some 600 Soviet tanks and 200 Soviet jet aircraft. These figures, as indeed all figures about weapon numbers, are approximations (which in this case are thought to be close approximations). It should be noted that losses of weapons by accident and, more important, effective reduction of weapon numbers caused by excessively long repair times and shortage of trained operators, are not allowed for in the above figures, which relate to deliveries rather than numbers in operation.

The Egyptian tank stock consisted of T34 models surviving from 1956 or supplied as replacements, together with their successors, the T54 and T55 series, numbering about 500 units. There were also about 50 Iosif Stalin Mark III heavy tanks

ABOVE: *The Egyptian Army's new Soviet T54 tanks parade through Cairo, 1966.*
LEFT: *A military parade in Cairo in July 1959, showing a Model 1937 152mm gun and an Su-100 assault gun.*

and 150-odd SU-100 self-propelled guns. About 50 PT-76 light tanks were also available. Syria had a mix of T34 and T54 models, with about 50 SU-100s, and Iraq had perhaps 400 T34s and T54s, although a high proportion of these were on the non-operation list. Thus, in terms of tanks delivered, Israel was considerably outnumbered by her enemies in 1967, having

BELOW: Israel's most modern warplane on the eve of the Six Day War was the Dassault Mirage III, supplied by France.
BOTTOM: An Egyptian Navy Komar-class FPB fires a Styx antiship missile.

perhaps 1100 tanks and self-propelled guns to match the 2000 or so units held by Egypt, Syria and Iraq (not to speak of the 300 units possessed by Jordan). On the other hand, in terms of tanks available for service, the disparity was considerably less than these figures suggest. In terms of quality, the Soviet T54 and T55 models were formidable, but Israel's acquisition of a number of British Centurion tanks, probably superior to any other tanks in this region in practical as opposed to theoretical abilities, served to balance this. After the first T54s had been delivered to Egypt, Israel attempted to acquire M-48

Patton tanks from the USA, and a scheme was worked out by which West Germany would hand on such units to Israel (thereby relieving the USA of apparent collusion in the deal). However, Arab governments threatened West Germany with various retaliatory measures and the project was abandoned, but the USA then agreed to supply the units direct. The M-48 was outgunned by the T54 and T55 (90mm main gun against 100mm) and was slower and of shorter cruising range. But the Soviet designs were uncomfortable to operate (hence, among other things, had a slower rate of fire and tended to be less

accurate in their gunfire) so were probably not a match for the M-48. The Centurion, although slower than the Soviet designs, was plainly a superior weapon, with an excellent gun. In later years Israel rearmed many of its tanks, including surviving Shermans and captured Soviet models, with the Vickers 105mm gun as used in the Centurions. On the whole, Israel had a larger proportion of older tanks still in first-line service than did her enemies.

The course of events in 1967 determined that the quality and number of tanks in the possession of the belligerents was of little relevance to the outcome of the war. It was air power which was the decisive factor. The number and types of aircraft which the USSR delivered (and equally the types which the Russians refused to deliver) emphasize that the underlying Soviet intention was to rearm Egypt in order that Nasser and his allies might be strong enough to pursue their revolutionizing (and ultimately anti-Western) objectives in the Middle East without, however, becoming so strong as to place the very existence of Israel in jeopardy. Despite Israeli allegations, which later became Israeli beliefs, that the Western powers would have simply stood by and watched the destruction of Israel in 1967, Moscow realized that such a possibility would most likely have brought American intervention and thereby a possible US-Soviet armed conflict, and Moscow's first priority was to avoid such a conflict. The pattern of aircraft deliveries gave a clear indication, ignored by the Western press but possibly quietly understood in Western defense departments, of Soviet intentions.

On the eve of the 1967 war the Egyptian inventory of Soviet aircraft was (again approximately) 120 fighter-bombers of the MiG-15 types and its successor the MiG-

ABOVE: *The standard Israeli surface-to-air missile in 1967 was the Raytheon MIM-23 Hawk, pictured on its mobile launcher.*

17, 60 MiG-19 all-weather fighters that could also serve as fighter-bombers, 130 MiG-21 supersonic fighters, a handful of SU-7 fighter-bombers, 40 IL-28 light bombers, and 30 TU-16 medium bombers. The weakness of the medium bomber force, just enough to present the possibility of a strike against Israeli cities but not enough to make such strikes terrifying, is noteworthy, as is the heavy emphasis on aircraft suitable for short-range interception and ground attack. The whole pattern of the air force built under Soviet auspices suggests a force which could counter Israeli air attacks against targets on Egyptian territory and at the same time prevent a repetition of the 1956 circumstance of overwhelming Israeli advantage in ground-support air activity over the battlefield. The supply of SAM-2 antiaircraft missiles can be seen as another essentially defensive move, designed to prevent Israeli air mastery without opening Israel to really destructive bombardment. In fact, Khrushchev had earlier refused an Egyptian request for surface-to-surface missiles which, his experts warned him, could have been used to bombard Israeli cities from sites in the Gaza Strip. Soviet refusal to create a Middle Eastern surface-to-surface missile capability outside its own control is also, presumably, the explanation of its failure to help the

ABOVE: *An Israeli tank crew wait beside their M-50 Super Sherman, 1967.*
LEFT: *Twin-engined Sud Vautour attack aircraft were the only Israeli warplanes with sufficient range to attack airfields in southern Egypt.*
BELOW: *An Israeli soldier mans his weapons pit in May 1967, shortly before the outbreak of the Six Day War.*

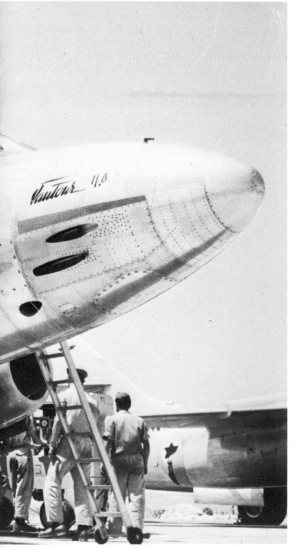

Egyptians with their medium-range missiles, domestically designed and built. These had been produced by German technicians attracted by the Egyptian government, but were ineffective because of problems with their guidance systems. The Russians could have remedied these problems, but refrained from doing so. Soviet aircraft deliveries to Syria and Iraq were not dissimilar; Iraq received a handful of TU-16 bombers, but Syria did not, and both had IL-28 twin-engined bombers in small numbers. But the emphasis was on MiG-17, MiG-19, and MiG-21 interceptors and fighter-bombers.

As with tanks, the Israelis were considerably outnumbered in aircraft by their hostile neighbors, although the actual, operational, discrepancy was considerably less marked than the nominal, inventory, difference. In general, because of the reluctance of Western governments to disturb what they termed the balance in the Middle East, Israeli acquisitions usually followed deliveries of Soviet aircraft to her enemies, these deliveries being used to persuade the West that Israel needed something to restore the balance. Thus, for example, a 1958 delivery of French Vautour twin-engine bombers followed a delivery of IL-28 bombers to Egypt. France was the principal supplier of aircraft; its government, except for a short and painful period during the de Gaulle regime, usually maintained a sympathetic relationship with Israel. When in the early 1960s the Mirage III aircraft was acquired, the Israelis decided that the payload of this supersonic fighter-bomber was sufficient to enable the Air Force to dispense with light bombers and concentrate on the acquisition of multi-purpose fighter-bombers that could be used for interception, bombing raids and ground support. As for the threat posed by the Egyptian medium bombers, this was countered by persuading the US government to permit the supply of Hawk antiaircraft missiles. A large proportion of these missiles were stationed to protect the Israeli atomic research station at Dimona, an interesting indication of the Israeli perception of how vulnerable and vital such stations might prove. On the eve of the 1967 war Israel had also put about 20 Super Mystère fighters into service, and was seeking to acquire more of these aircraft as well as more US Sky-hawks for ground attack work.

At sea, what the USSR supplied might be regarded as out of tune with the defense-orientation of the air and land weapons. In particular, the supply to Egypt of 36 guided-missile gunboats of the *Komar* and *Osa* series potentially put a very effective weapon into Egyptian hands. However, the short range of these boats, their vulnerability to air strikes, and perhaps an insufficient realization of their effectiveness, could explain this. The destroyers and submarines supplied to Egypt were not of modern type and were regarded as units which would present additional problems for the Israelis without presenting a major threat. At the time, the West was more worried about the base facilities which Soviet workers were constructing on Egypt's Mediterranean shore. It was felt that such bases could be used by the Red Navy, which was already showing signs of a wish to establish a permanent squadron in the Mediterranean to offset the advantage enjoyed in diplomacy and saber-rattling by the USA, with its powerful Sixth Fleet.

Soviet military advisers were well aware of the deficiencies of the Egyptian armed forces, and realized that for the Egyptian forces to have any chance of success against the Israelis they would have to enjoy a substantial preponderance both of men and weapons. The Egyptians, and the combined Egyptian, Syrian, and Iraqi forces, did not have sufficient preponderance, and that is how the USSR wished the situation to remain. But whereas the Soviet experts could see that Nasser was in no condition to rout the Israelis, this Nasser himself refused to accept.

RIGHT: *Egyptian self-propelled ZSU-57-2 AA guns.*
BELOW: *Israeli artillerymen emplace a 155mm howitzer to face Syria.*

BELOW: *Israeli Super Sherman tanks advancing in the Sinai, 7 June 1982.*

THE SIX DAY WAR
-1967-

The series of mistakes and misapprehensions leading directly to the 1967 war began in 1966. In that year, incursions into Israel by Palestinian raiders from Syrian territory noticeably increased, putting at risk the lives of the inhabitants cultivating the soil of that part of Israel adjoining Syria. Israel actually appealed to the Soviet government to use its influence with the Syrians to discourage these incursions, but the Soviet reply was to suggest that frontier incidents were being contrived by Western intelligence services in order to provoke bigger conflicts. This might well have reflected a genuine Soviet belief; having established their influence in Syria, the Russians would have expected the Western powers to seek to damage the Syrian regime, and the easiest way of doing so would have been to encourage the Israelis to attack, and even invade, Syria. But whatever the degree of Soviet sincerity, a satisfactory Russian response to the Israeli appeal was obviously unlikely at the time, and the appeal was made not with any hope of success but to prepare the way for later Israeli action, which was diplomatic as much as military.

Israel's position worsened in that year because Egypt and Syria, having quarrelled at the time of Syria's departure from union with Egypt, were repairing their relationship. In fact, in November they made a new military agreement which appeared to strengthen the military capability of both partners and to present a threat to Israel of a two-front conflict. This agreement was applauded by Moscow, which was well aware of how co-operation and co-ordination between what it regarded as progressive Arab states (by that time Egypt, Syria, Iraq and Algeria) would increase their, and Moscow's, influence in the Middle East. It might have

been a new sense of nervousness, leading to the decision to make a demonstration of strength, that persuaded the Israeli government to carry out a very strong retaliatory raid on a Jordanian village, combined with a more emphatic artillery and small-arms response to attacks from Syria. Then, in early April 1967, Israeli aircraft attacking Syrian artillery positions found themselves in battle over the Sea of Galilee with Syrian aircraft. This resulted in a clear victory for the Israelis, who claimed the destruction of six Syrian fighters with no losses on the Israeli side. That the Syrian fighters were the very latest supplied by the USSR, MiG-21s, would alone have caused disquiet in Moscow, for the battle suggested that the latest Soviet weapons were inferior to those supplied to Israel by the West (in this case, Mystère fighters obtained from France).

Having reflected on all this, and evidently concluding that both Soviet and Egyptian influence needed a boost in the Middle East, the Soviet government condemned Israel, suggesting that it was playing the American game and that the USSR was very concerned at the Israeli-launched disturbances so close to the USSR. This geographical inexactitude suggests that the Soviet condemnation was more of a gesture than an expression of genuine alarm. It was followed by Soviet assertions that Israel was concentrating troops near the Syrian border, in what looked like preparations for an invasion. This assertion was false, and UN observers later made clear it was false, and in May the Soviet ambassador to Israel refused an invitation to visit the area to see that there was no Israeli concentration there. Whether the USSR was misinformed, disinformed or was deliberately fabricating the evidence it needed

is immaterial, for the result would have been the same in any case. The most likely explanation of Soviet behavior is that misinformation began the affair, and the concept of an Israeli concentration so fitted Moscow's preconceptions that it was difficult for the Soviet government to abandon the idea.

Whether or not the Russians believed this story, it had the effect they wanted, of compelling Nasser to assert himself as leader of the progressive Arabs. Helped perhaps by Israeli Arabic broadcasts, Arabs began to wonder whether Nasser, secure behind the cover provided by the United Nations peacekeeping force (UNEF), was leaving the Syrians to their fate. To maintain his prestige, and therefore his own position, it was necessary for Nasser to assert himself against Israel. This had been the Soviet aim, but before long Nasser ran out of control so far as Russian diplomacy was concerned.

At the end of April, Anwar Sadat, who was paying a visit to Moscow as a close associate of Nasser, was told by the Soviet prime minister that Russian intelligence had clear information that the Israelis were massing close to the Syrian frontier. Evidently, at this stage the USSR was persuading Nasser to assert himself, and when on 14 May Nasser put his forces on the alert and moved large formations into Sinai, it was probably with Soviet approval. But Nasser's next move probably was not.

What Nasser did two days later was to request the UN to remove its peacekeeping troops from some points of the Egypt-Israel frontier, the request later being amended to include the UN presence at Sharm El-Sheikh. The UN Secretary-General, U Thant, in a decision for which he was savagely criticized at the time and later, decided to withdraw all UN forces. Subsequently, this was held to have opened the way for the 1967 war, and U Thant has been variously condemned for cowardice and ineptitude. This judgment remains general, although it is possible that one day U Thant's action will be seen as rational and courageous. It was rational because it recognized what world statesmen and their spokesmen refused to recognize, that in the absence of agreement from both sides the UN force would be too weak to prevent war. It was little more than an observer force in any case, and had been accepted in 1956 because both Israel and Egypt wanted a peace settlement and a simultaneous assurance that the other side would observe that agreement. With Nasser already having 100,000 troops in Sinai and apparently on the warpath, the UN force became an irrelevance. U Thant recognized this, and those

LEFT: *Troops of the United Nations Emergency Force parade at the King's Gate checkpoint, 1967. This provided access to the Gaza strip from Israeli territory.*

statesmen who later chose him as a suitable scapegoat showed no enthusiasm, at the time or earlier, for installing a UN force which would actually have some fighting capacity. U Thant's acceptance of reality was not an act of cowardice.

Concentration of Egyptian troops in Sinai, ejection of the UN force, Egyptian resumption of their strongpoint at Sharm El-Sheikh, from where they again blocked shipping attempting to reach the Israeli port of Eilat, were moves which Israel obviously could not ignore. The rest of the world, including Moscow, was also apprehensive. A few weeks before Nasser had been passing through a period of relative unpopularity and insecurity. With his seemingly never-ending campaign in the Yemen and his needlessly vituperative relationships with the kings of Saudi Arabia and Jordan, he had seemed impotent. From this feeling of impotence the USSR had pushed him into an aggressive posture and Nasser suddenly discovered he was once again the idol of the Arab masses. With this change in his fortunes he would, once again, be tempted to push his luck too far.

The Soviet and US governments were in contact during April and May, and their exchanges were not especially acrimonious, as both wished to preserve the peace, without, however, weakening their own positions in the Middle East. The perceived need to support Nasser publicly, and to a certain stage in private, made it hard for Moscow to restrain him. It does seem that Soviet efforts were made to persuade Nasser not to blockade the Strait

RIGHT: *(l-r) Generals Bar-Lev, Sharon and Gavish arrive at a desert airstrip in the Negev by Sikorsky S-58 helicopter.*
BELOW: *Israel's Minister of Defense, Moshe Dayan, gives a press conference.*

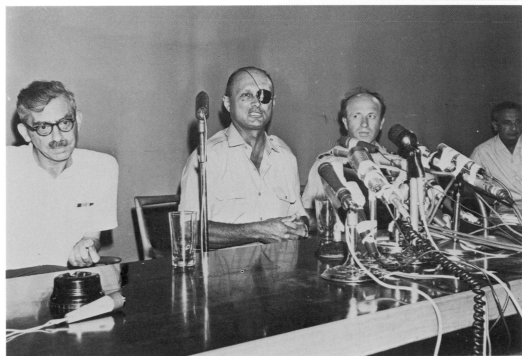

of Tiran from Sharm El-Sheikh, and not to concentrate his army on Israel's frontier, but these appeals had no success. Nasser further bolstered his position when his recent arch-enemy, King Hussein of Jordan, having calculated that Egypt was on the brink of defeating Israel, decided it would be politic to swallow his pride and join in on Egypt's side. The result was a Jordanian-Egyptian military agreement reached at the end of May. This made Israel's survival beyond a few more weeks seem even more questionable.

From 17 May, when Nasser's troop moves to Sinai were actually announced, the Israeli government abandoned its previous nonchalant poise and sought ways to avert the threat. Dayan, who at that time held no military post, was one of those urging immediate violent action on the grounds that the IDF could still beat the Egyptians, but that time was not on Israel's side. In his memoirs Dayan suggests that Prime Minister Levi Eshkol

ABOVE: *Southern sector Israeli commanders confer with General Gavish (center).*
LEFT: *The Six Day War opened with devastating Israeli airstrikes on Egyptian airfields on 5 June. Three burned out MiG-21s are pictured.*

lacked boldness at this point, but Eshkol was probably intent on exhausting diplomatic action before embarking on military gambles. However, diplomacy produced nothing concrete from Washington, while Paris decided that a pro-Arab attitude was more advantageous; possibly the end of the Algerian war, which had provoked tension between Egypt and France, was one reason for this change of tack. Keeping its reserves mobilized over a long period was damaging to the already fragile Israeli economy, but the Eshkol government was unable to decide whether or not to launch a pre-emptive attack on Egypt. Egypt, apart from enrolling Jordan to join the Egypt-Iraq-Syria alliance, had also been promised detachments from other Arab states, including Algeria. It is said that the Israeli Chief of Staff (Yitzhak Rabin) collapsed at this point from excessive cigarette consumption, being temporarily replaced by Ezer Weizman. The main significance of this two-day disablement is that the Israeli command was in a state

of high tension at this time, being preoccupied not only by the actions of neighboring Arab governments, but also by what seemed like lack of action by its own. Certainly the Israeli public at large, and its press, began to show signs of impatience with Eshkol, who finally formed a new multiparty government which included the former leader of the opposition (Menachem Begin) and, more important, a new Defense Minister, Moshe Dayan.

With Dayan as Defense Minister the decision to make a pre-emptive attack was finally confirmed. Dayan was right, insofar as Nasser had done two things which Israel had always regarded as justifying armed action. He had once more closed the Strait of Tiran to Israeli shipping, and he had formed an offensive military alliance with states bordering Israel. Nor had he made any secret of his intentions. Indeed on 26 May he made a speech to Arab trade unionists in which the destruction of Israel was clearly envisaged. The agreement with Jordan was followed by the dispatch of the Egyptian General Abdal Riadh to take over the Jordanian forces. In the conditions of Arab material preponderance, it seemed to the Israeli command that a pre-emptive strike, facing the Egyptians and their allies with an unexpected circumstance right at

the beginning, was the only way out.

The war that started on 5 June 1967 has since been named the Six Day War; logically enough, in view of its duration. In fact, its outcome was decided in just one day, the first. At breakfast time on that day almost the entire Israeli Air Force was dispatched against Egyptian military airfields in Sinai, along the Suez Canal and Red Sea, and certain Nile Delta and Nile Valley sites. Most of the Egyptian Air Force officers seem to have been caught between home and base in these attacks; pilots who managed to reach their aircraft were for the most part killed or injured when they were struck as they sought to take off. These Israeli attacks were the result of meticulous planning by the Air Force, headed by its commander Mordecai Hod, and were provided with excellent intelligence about Egyptian dispositions. In three hours that morning the entire Egyptian medium bomber force was destroyed, and most of the light bombers were put out of action too. This onslaught on the Egyptian TU-16 and IL-28 squadrons must have been a great relief for the Israelis, who no longer needed to devote resources for protection against bombing raids on cities. In addition, a high proportion of the SU-7 aircraft were eliminated. Of the Egyptian MiG-17, -19 and -21 aircraft, more than half were destroyed. In total, of about 500 firstline aircraft, the Egyptians lost about 300.

There was an element of gamble in the Israeli onslaught. Counting on initial inaction on the part of Egypt's allies, only 12 of the Israeli fighters were left behind to defend the airspace over Israeli territory. Taking a precaution that the Egyptians had failed to take, these defending aircraft during those vulnerable hours were deployed so that two-thirds were always in the air while the remaining four were being refueled at the ends of their runways.

The few Egyptian aircraft that managed to get into the air were soon shot down, but a few Israeli aircraft were lost also, and the Egyptian pilots were not lacking in boldness. It is usual for attacks on airfields to produce greater losses in aircraft than in pilots, and this was the case on 5 June. Egypt suddenly found itself with considerably more pilots than aircraft. If the USSR had acceded to Egyptian requests for immediate replacement aircraft the war might, just possibly, have ended differently, but Moscow refused to

help in this way. As in the days preceding the war, Moscow wanted peace, and realized that supplying replacement arms to Egypt would only prolong the war.

Factors which contributed to the destructiveness of the Israeli Air Force's early-morning visitation included the circumstance that the Egyptians had neither dispersed their aircraft on the airfields nor placed a suitable proportion of their machines in safe rear airbases beyond the effective range of their enemy. It is unlikely that their Soviet advisers would have neglected to recommend these procedures; after all, at Port Arthur in 1904 and along the Soviet-German frontier in 1941 the Russian forces had already experienced the destruction of surprise onslaughts, and indeed the 1941 disaster of the Red Air Force had much in common with the 1967 experience of the Egyptian. So there is probably some truth in the Soviet assertion that the Egyptians refused to take good advice. On 5 June 1967 there was not the slightest advantage in having the Egyptian bombers so close to Israel and the advanced fighters were more

numerous than was required to deal with an Israeli bombing attack on Egyptian territory.

It is likely that those Egyptian pilots who at the time of the attack were actually on duty had just returned to their airfields from night patrols. Air bases that for one reason or another were not attacked by the Israelis did not dispatch their aircraft to the aid of those that were. Whether this was a procedural shortcoming or a result of communication problems is not clear, but it certainly eased the work of the Israeli pilots. Furthermore, even in the absence of these factors the discrepancy between Israeli and Egyptian numbers would have been irrelevant in this morning's activities in view of the thoughtful design of Israeli aircraft and weapon systems, and their proficiency in refueling, rearming and turning around their machines. Most Israeli aircraft were ready for action within 15 minutes of returning to their bases, whereas Egyptian ground

BELOW: *Israeli tank crews scramble to man their Centurions in the Negev.*

crews needed about two hours. Hence the Israeli Air Force seemed several times stronger than it actually was, and this may have persuaded the Egyptian command that American aircraft, from US aircraft carriers, were also engaged. Later, Nasser and Hussein concocted a story that American aircraft had indeed been responsible for the Israeli success. However, after Israeli intelligence sources published a transcript of the radio conversation on this subject between Nasser and Hussein, the latter admitted that the allegation was false.

Hussein's air force seems to have been the first to come to the aid of Nasser, making light but symbolically valuable raids on Israeli airfields at Natanya, Kfar Sirkin and Kfar Sava. Much later, the Syrians managed to dispatch bombers to the Haifa oil installations and another Israeli airfield. The next day, a solitary Iraqi TU-16 reached Israel, dropped a few bombs on Natanya, and was then shot down. It seems clear that there was no effective defense co-ordination between the high commands of the warring Arab states. Lack of co-ordination was a result of inter-Arab suspicions and rivalries, and closer relations were probably not encouraged by the Russian advisers, for political reasons.

Considerable time separated the beginning of the Israeli air attack on Egypt and the moment when the Israeli command felt that the Egyptian Air Force had suffered enough, and that the time was right to turn attention toward the air forces of Egypt's allies. By the end of that first day almost the entire Jordanian Air Force (whose main force had been about 20 Hunter fighters) had been destroyed, as had the bulk of the Syrian Air Force. Strikes against the Iraqi Air Force were limited to one airfield, known as H3. Henceforth the Israeli Air Force was able to concentrate its attention on ground support, and this determined the fate of the Egyptian and Syrian troops. In the course of the war it would seem that fewer than 50 Israeli aircraft were lost, mostly from ground fire. The SAM-2 missile installations of the Egyptians and Syrians proved ineffective, for Israeli air operations were conducted so close to the ground that these surface-to-air missiles could not be used with any hope of success.

After 5 June, therefore, the war settled down to a rapidly moving series of ground battles whose course was determined by Israeli air superiority. This superiority not only permitted destructive air attacks on Arab formations, but prevented similar attacks being made on Israeli troops. The speed of Israeli advances, especially in Sinai, owed much to the security in which supplies, especially of fuel, could be brought up to the advancing units. In turn, the rapidity of the advance threw the opposing command completely off

ABOVE. *Israeli operations in the Sinai during the Six Day War, June 1967.*

balance so what started as an Egyptian retreat ended as a rout. Throughout this week, efforts to restore peace were being made in the United Nations and elsewhere. Both the USA and the USSR wanted peace (and used their new 'hot line' for the first time in exchanging ideas), so available time was short for an Israeli victory which would provide the foundation for a peace which, better than the 1956 agreement, would guarantee the country's basic needs for survival. Once again the IDF was engaged in a triumphant but anxiety-fraught race against time. Meanwhile, Russian advisers in Syria and Egypt were withdrawn out of harm's way, leaving their protégés to proceed as best they could. Contrary to press statements of that time, no Soviet personnel, dead or alive, fell into Israeli hands.

At sea, despite the naval craft at Egypt's disposition, the war brought little excitement. The main event occurred at the same time as the final ceasefire, when a US electronic intelligence vessel, the *Liberty*, placidly gathering information off the Israeli coast, was attacked by Israeli aircraft and suffered many casualties. The *Liberty* was presumably listening to the transmissions of both sides, with a view to obtaining information about the real situation, as opposed to what the belligerents claimed was happening. The suggestion that it knew rather too much about various Israeli deceptions (largely aimed at confusing Israel's enemies with fake transmissions appearing to emanate from Cairo and other Arab communication centers) was probably true, but the suggestion that this is why the Israelis attacked seems unconvincing. As always in military puzzles, muddle is the most likely explanation. The incident did little to disturb US-Israeli relations; Israel eventually offered compensation but did not admit to any feeling of guilt. Elsewhere at

LEFT: *General Gavish was GOC Southern Command in the Six Day War.*
RIGHT: *General Tal (right).*

tians themselves had made during the intervening years were sufficient to ensure that this campaign could not be exactly like that of 1956. Apart from constructing camps and supply depots, and fortified areas stronger than those of 1956, the Egyptians had improved the road system so that connections between the main west-east routes were more numerous. They had also opened up the Gidi Pass, north of the Mitla Pass, to provide an alternative route for vehicles proceeding to and from the Suez area.

In Sinai, Israel's troops were commanded by Yeshayahu Gavish, and his men were divided into three task forces of divisional size. Israel Tal's force was in the north, ready to move along the Mediterranean coast while at the same time taking care of the Gaza Strip. A little to the south was Abraham Yoffe's force, which was to advance over soft desert (regarded as virtually impassable by the Egyptians) to Bir Lafan, where it would be in a good position to assist either the northern or the southern task force by attacking the Egyptians from an unexpected direction. To the south, Arik Sharon's force was to tackle the fortified zones centered on Um Katef and Abu Ageila, while making a supplementary thrust southeastward to the key road junction of Nakhle. Briefly, the Israeli intention was to crack the hard nuts represented by the Rafah and Abu Ageila defenses, throwing the defenders off balance by attacking from unanticipated directions. Having thereby created safe gaps through which to advance, the Israeli forces would destroy Egyptian formations in the rear before they had time to organize themselves. Then, without wasting time over the capture of strongly defended bases, the Israelis would move rapidly toward the Suez Canal, spread themselves along its length, so as to cut off the Egyptian retreat and force the Egyptian armor to fight in unfavorable conditions. On the whole these objectives were achieved, although casualties were heavier than in 1956. Israeli casualties were about 1400 in Sinai, of which about 300 were fatal. However, Egyptian casualties were about 10 times larger than this, and their material losses were enormous.

The initial, breakthrough, phase of the Israeli plan was completed in two days. It was here that the heaviest casualties were suffered, for the Egyptian soldiers fought gallantly and effectively, aided by their long-prepared defense systems. A few minutes after the Israeli Air Force appeared over Egypt's airfields, Tal's 7th Armored Brigade, skirting minefields, struck at the junction of the two infantry divisions defending Rafah, while a parachute brigade under Eitan with tanks in

sea, Egyptian submarines appear to have approached the Israel coast and been scared off by depth charges, but there was no effective action by surface ships.

The land war resolved itself into three theaters, the campaign in Sinai, and the operations against Syria and Jordan. The Sinai operations had first priority for Israel, and it was only after the Egyptians were safely in flight that the other theaters were opened up. Nevertheless, the campaign against Syria finally absorbed more Israeli effort, at least from the air, than the Sinai campaign. This was partly because Israel wished to build a position in this region that would prevent a recurrence of the *Fedayeen* and official Syrian attacks and incursions that had preceded this war. The capture of the Golan Heights, from which Syrian guns had frequently shelled Israeli farms, was a significant Israeli war aim. The need to win the required victory over the Syrians delayed Israel's acceptance of a ceasefire and thereby aroused a flurry of half-veiled threats from the USSR.

Thanks to air strikes, the occasions on which Arab and Israeli tank forces got to grips were less frequent than had been anticipated. In general, the Israeli's better training and the superior operating qualities of most of their tanks gave them a battle-winning advantage. The Centurions in particular proved their worth, being

able to engage the Egyptian T54 and T55 tanks outside the latters' gun range. The Arab antitank guns were served by well-trained troops, but they lacked the mobility required to deal with the wide-ranging Israeli tanks. The *Shmel'* antitank missile supplied by the USSR did not achieve good results.

The largest tank encounters occurred in the first day or so, before the Israeli aerial preponderance was brought into play. In Sinai the Egyptians had two armored divisions in support of their five infantry divisions. Intended eventually to lead an Egyptian offensive, at the time of the Israeli pre-emptive strike one of these two divisions was stationed in the rear – the elite 4th Armored Division, located near Bir Gafgafa. 'Force Shazli,' a division-size armored formation was poised along the frontier between Kuntilla and Kusseima, its eventual aim being a thrust right across to the Jordanian frontier so as to cut off the southern Negev and Eilat from the rest of Israel. On the whole, though, the Egyptian deployment was similar to that of 1956, while geography determined that the Israeli movements were largely a repetition of that earlier campaign. However, the Egyptian command mistakenly anticipated that the Israelis would simply duplicate their 1956 plan of operations. In fact, the infrastructural improvements that the Egyp-

support made an outflanking sweep in the south of the Egyptian positions, and then swept into the defending gun batteries. This reduction of the Rafah defenses took the best part of the day, but before nightfall on 5 June the 7th Brigade had captured Sheikh Zuweid to the west, where its Patton and Centurion tanks had little difficulty in overcoming a battalion of T34 units. During the night of 5/6 June, Tal's forces consolidated positions at El-Arish preparatory to a final occupation of that town the following morning. After this, part moved toward the Suez Canal around Kantara, while a tank force was sent south to secure the El Arish airfield and Bir Lahfan, a settlement commanding the road to Abu Ageila, which at that time was being occupied by Sharon's task force.

Sharon's force had both the most essential and the most difficult task in these two days. It was required not only to defeat the defending concentrations, but also to ensure Israeli control of the west-east highway from Ismailia to Nitzana. On 5 June, after crushing an outer Egyptian defense position at Tarat Um-Basis, Sharon advanced on to the Um-Katef and Abu Ageila fortified zones. While his artillery executed a prolonged bombardment, a strong armored reconnaissance was made to the north, again over soft desert sand that the defenders had regarded as impassable. Despite some heavy fighting, this group managed to pass to the north of Abu Ageila and take the road junctions controlling the routes toward El Arish and Jebel Libni. Sharon had

dispatched another force to cover the road from Abu Ageila to Kusseima, so Abu Ageila was completely cut off from reinforcement. Still on the first day, after dark, helicopters carried paratroopers to the Egyptian rear with the aim, successfully achieved, of dealing with the defending artillery. Sharon's main force of tanks and infantry attacked from the east and by dawn the whole complex was in Israeli hands, although fighting in and around the Egyptian trenches had been bitter and heavy.

Meanwhile Yoffe's task force, plowing over soft sand dunes between and parallel to Tal's and Sharon's advances, was achieving its main objective of preventing any north-south movement (that is, lateral to the advance) on the part of Egyptian

reinforcing units. If the Egyptians had been able to swing formations between the Tal and Sharon fronts in accordance with the hour-by-hour situation, the Israeli task would have been considerably more difficult. By reaching Bir Lahfan late on the second day, Yoffe's men commanded a road junction which enabled them to achieve their object. When an Egyptian armored force moved from the Ismailia area toward Jebel Libni it was confronted by Yoffe's tanks ensconced in protected positions alongside the Bir Lahfan junction, and routed.

It was toward the end of the second day that the Egyptian nerve showed signs of breaking. This was not simply a consequence of the perilous tactical situation in which the Egyptian forces were placed in Sinai, but resulted also from the psychological strain of not knowing exactly what was going on while being increasingly aware that something disastrous was happening. Field Marshal Amer committed suicide after the war rather than face a trial in which it was evident he would be portrayed, rightly or wrongly, as the main cause of the defeat. He did not leave behind fellow-officers willing to defend his reputation. Earlier, he had enjoyed the trust of Nasser, and had been entrusted with the conduct of the war in the Yemen, a campaign which hardly covered him with glory. In the Sinai operations of June 1967 he is said to have lost his nerve and issued conflicting and confusing orders which turned Egyptian discomfiture into a military catastrophe. He is said, too, to have been addicted to drugs. No doubt many of these allegations came from the army's and government's obvious need for a scapegoat, but there were certainly some pointed questions that needed to be asked about his conduct. One of these concerns the information he was sending back to Cairo about the first day's fighting. In Cairo, and in other Arab cities, crowds assembled to cheer the great Egyptian victories that were being reported. When, a couple of days later, the truth became obvious, both the Army and Nasser himself felt a backlash of disappointed fury on the part of the public. This was not an irrecoverable situation for Nasser, for as the situation worsened the public's feeling that he was the only man likely to turn defeat into victory ensured him con-

BELOW: *Egyptian Air Force MiG-17s carry out a strafing attack on an Israeli convoy heading toward the Suez Canal.*

BELOW: *Burned out Egyptian transport, destroyed by IDF Air Force strafing, line the road through the Mitla Pass.*

tinuing support, but the popular feeling against the Army continued, and no doubt was a reason for the courts-martial of leading officers afterward. Meanwhile, Nasser was telling his allies in Damascus, Amman, and Baghdad that the Israelis were being defeated and that his Shazli Division was even then approaching the

Israeli-Jordanian frontier. It was this optimistic assessment that persuaded King Hussein, despite his misgivings, to throw his forces whole-heartedly into battle.

It has been suggested that *Mossad* (the Israeli secret intelligence organization) had a hand in this. Having broken Egyptian cyphers, it is said, the Israelis caught

Egyptian radio messages, changed them to convey a highly optimistic report of Egyptian successes, and then retransmitted them to their original destinations. No solid evidence has been produced for these claims, and the banal explanation, that Amer and his officers were unwilling to report bad news, or at least delayed sending it in the hope that it might be overtaken by better tidings, seems much more plausible. Whatever the explanation, throughout this war Nasser seems to have been unaware at each stage of how bad the situation was. It was not until late afternoon on the first day, for example, that he realized that for most practical purposes his air force had ceased to exist. A few days later, aware that the situation was grim but unaware of its catastrophic grimness, he delayed agreement to a ceasefire in the hope of improving his position by a last-minute success.

On 6 June Gaza was captured by an Israeli reserve infantry brigade against stiff and prolonged resistance; most of the remainder of the Gaza Strip had been overrun earlier the same day, with infantry and paratroops combining to capture the hill dominating Gaza town. On 7 June, with Israeli Air Force ground-attack operations getting into full swing, Tal's men pushed westward, with one arm assisting Yoffe's men to capture the supply base of Bir Gafgafa and one brigade pushing toward the northern end of the Suez Canal. It was in defense of Bir Gafgafa that the Egyptians launched their last substantial counterattack by tanks; this was defeated. Yoffe's force moved on toward the Mitla and Gidi passes, through which

LEFT: *A captured Egyptian soldier is helped aboard the boat returning him home.*
BOTTOM LEFT: *Israeli troops in Gaza.*
BELOW: *The Egyptian governor of Gaza, Gen Abdul Hussaini, is led into captivity.*

RIGHT: *An Israeli gunboat patrols off Sharm-el-Sheikh in the Straits of Tiran.*
BELOW RIGHT: *A map of Israeli operations on the West Bank of the River Jordan.*

it seemed likely that the cut-off Egyptian formations would seek to withdraw westward. An advance unit of nine Israeli tanks made a rush to the eastern end of the Mitla Pass so as to block it. In doing so, four of its tanks ran out of fuel but were towed to their destination by the others. Here they were bedded down in defensive positions and succeeded in holding up the Egyptians for several crucial hours; they were eventually relieved by other tanks after having let pass only one Egyptian tank during their lone battle.

The movements of other Israeli formations had the effect of pushing the escaping Egyptian formations toward the two passes, the eastern approaches to which became a killing ground for Israeli armor, guns, and especially aircraft and napalm. Hundreds of Egyptian tanks and thousands of other vehicles met their end here.

Meanwhile an Egyptian attempt to launch an armored counterattack so as to hold back the Israelis from the Canal was disturbed by Tal's leading formation of AMX tanks. The latter, being lightly armored, wisely did not press an attack against the opposing T55 tanks, but maintained contact until heavier Israeli tanks arrived. The latter engaged in a long-range bombardment over the sand dunes and after a four-hour battle virtually destroyed the Egyptian formation.

On 8 June the two prongs of Tal's force, after passing, respectively, Kantara and Ismailia, linked up on the bank of the Canal. Together with Yoffe's forces, which had finished the Mitla engagement, they then went south to Suez.

On 7 June, a combined attack by the Army and Navy on Sharm El-Sheikh had proved something of an anticlimax. The troops were duly landed, but found Sharm El-Sheikh abandoned by the Egyptians.

On 8 June the ceasefire brought the Sinai operations to a formal close. In those few days, in this theater, the Egyptian Army had lost four-fifths of its equipment, including perhaps 800 tanks and thousands of vehicles. The Israelis captured enough serviceable Egyptian tanks to emerge from this war with a net gain for their tank inventory of a hundred or so units.

Operations on the Jordanian and Syrian fronts developed to their full intensity only some days after the start of hostilities. A carefully timed message was sent to King Hussein by Israel on 5 June. Dispatched so as to reach him while the Egyptian airfields were being attacked, it offered to spare Jordan any hostile acts so long as Jordan refrained from entering the war against Israel. Hussein's reply is said to have conveyed the message that Israel had, after all, attacked Egypt and that the Jor-

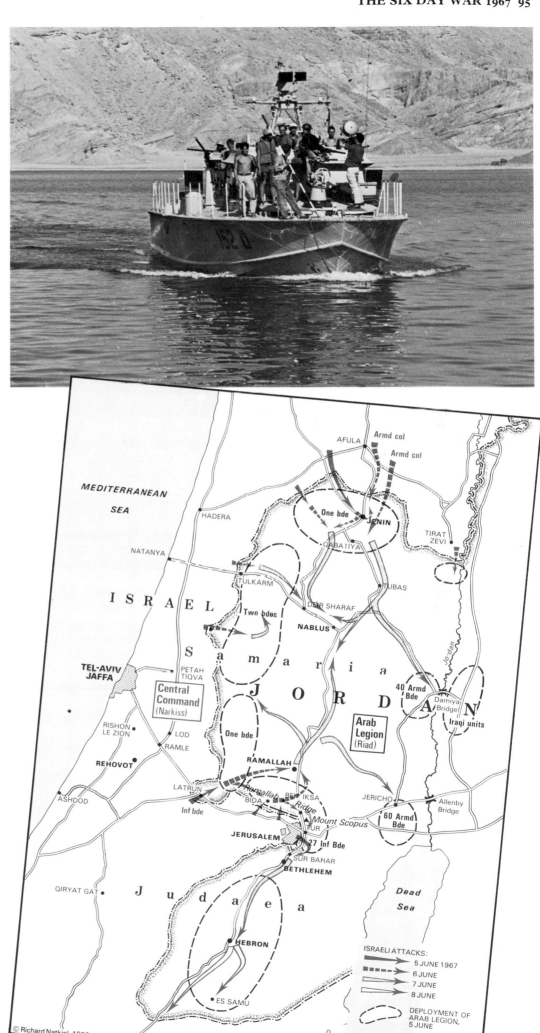

© Richard Natkiel, 1982

ISRAELI ATTACKS:
- - - 5 JUNE 1967
- - - 6 JUNE
— 7 JUNE
→ 8 JUNE

DEPLOYMENT OF ARAB LEGION, 5 JUNE

danian official reply to the Israeli message would be delivered by air; Hussein's Hunter fighters which attacked nearby Israeli airfields were Jordan's answer. At the same time, Jordanian artillery opened fire on Israeli airfields and towns. Israel's small size, and her convoluted frontiers, meant that Jordanian long-range guns could reach as far as Tel Aviv.

The small Jordanian Air Force was destroyed on its airfields within hours, but the land forces were not so easily dealt with. This sector, which the Israelis termed the Central Front, witnessed a week of determined fighting, both sides being aware that they were struggling over, and for, ancient land and towns that had been the cultural and spiritual nucleus of

RIGHT: *An Israeli paratroop scout unit moves cautiously through a deserted lane in the Old City of Jerusalem in June 1967.*

dence of the British High Commissioner in the days of the Palestine Mandate. Government House had been serving as the HQ of the UN Truce Supervision Organization, which was still in operation in this sector, and its capture by the Jordanians would seem to confirm that the UN forces had no chance of playing any effective role as soon as just one of the potential belligerents they were intended to supervise decided that it no longer wanted their services.

It had long been assumed that any hostilities with Jordan would be concerned exclusively with the West Bank, and the general Israeli plan had been worked out well in advance. The intention was to advance into Samaria from two directions (south from Nazareth and north from Jerusalem) while the Arab Legion in the west would be pinned down by holding attacks. Any Jordanian troops in Judea

both nations. Biblical settlements like Bethlehem, Jericho and Jerusalem itself were all encompassed in the Central Front.

That the Israelis hardly expected Hussein to make any other reply does not imply that their olive branch was hypocritical. They desperately wanted peace on this front, feeling that they could hardly fight Jordan at the same time as Egypt and Syria. However, it was soon clear that this is what they had to do and before that first day had passed Israeli units were in action against Jordan's Arab Legion. One of the first acts of the latter was an incursion into the demilitarized zone of Jerusalem, where it occupied Government House, the resi-

ABOVE: *An Israeli bazooka team take cover in the Old City of Jerusalem.*
RIGHT: *A motorized infantry unit moves through the Jordan hills.*
OPPOSITE: *Israeli infantry advance over high ground in Jerusalem.*

LEFT: *Moshe Dayan passes through the Lion's Gate into the Old City of Jerusalem.* RIGHT: *Israeli troops approach the Dome of Rock Mosque in the Old City.*

Shermans (rearmed with British 105mm guns) the Israeli armored units would have suffered considerably more had the Jordanians' communications and formations been less disturbed by air attack.

Meanwhile a reservist paratroop brigade which had been preparing for a drop in Sinai was diverted to the Central Front where, under Mordechai Gur, it was to capture the Arab sections of Jerusalem. Its successful redirection is a telling example of the flexibility and spontaneity which the IDF could display at this period. However, when Gur's men went into action during the night of 5/6 June, they did suffer from inadequate preparatory reconnaissance. Their first objective was the Jordanian Police School, which had been fortified and formed a strongpoint on the boundary separating the Jewish and Arab suburbs. Having to cut through four wire obstacles under fire, and then storm the Jordanian trenches, the paratroopers suffered quite severe casualties at this time. After overcoming this strongpoint they continued toward Ammunition Hill. This strongpoint was defended with well-emplaced machine guns, with the Jordanians in well-protected bunkers, and it was only at the price of another large casualty list that the Israelis were finally able to capture it at dawn. Twenty-one paratroopers were killed at Ammunition Hill, and most of the other soldiers were wounded; as things turned out, this was the hardest-fought engagement on the Central Front. The Jewish enclave on Mount Scopus, which had been isolated ever since the departure of the British, was once more made accessible by these paratroop night operations.

After this success, the Israelis prepared to cut the Jericho road, and thereby isolate Arab Jerusalem from the east. To do this it was first necessary to capture the Augusta Victoria building (between Mount Scopus and the Mount of Olives). However, despite the virtual impossibility of moving Jordanian reinforcements to Jerusalem (several relieving columns on the march were shattered by Israeli air attacks) the Jordanians in and around Jerusalem were still numerous and still battleworthy. Because of their effective resistance, the Israeli seizure of Augusta Victoria did not occur on 6 June, being postponed until the following day after the blocking Jordanian unit had withdrawn. Once taken, Augusta Victoria completed the isolation of the Arab sector of the city (the Old City). Gur's paratroopers rushed the Lions' Gate, giving access to the Old City, and moved through the Old City to the Western Wall. Meanwhile, from the other direction, the Jerusalem Brigade entered

were to be pressed toward the Dead Sea by Israeli forces moving south from Jerusalem. However, the initial Israeli move was directed toward expelling the Arab Legion from Government House, on the Hill of Evil Council. This was soon achieved by the Jerusalem Brigade, which then continued onward to capture Sur Bahir, commanding the road to Bethlehem, and thereby cutting off the Arab section of Jerusalem from Hebron as well as Bethlehem.

A reservists' armored brigade commanded by Uri Ben-Ari moved to the northern edge of the Israeli salient providing access to Jerusalem (the 'Jerusalem Corridor'), where it broke into Jordanian positions threatening the salient, capturing Maale Hahamishah and Sheikh Abdal-Azziz. After Beit Iksa was overrun by the Israelis they continued northward toward

Ramallah. Just south of that town, they encountered Jordanian armor and the resulting battle did nothing to discredit the Jordanians, even though in the end the Israelis prevailed. However, the Israelis had to engage in more severe fighting before they could take Ramallah, with its vital crossroads.

On the night of 5/6 June the police post at Latrun, which commanded the quickest route from Tel Aviv to Jerusalem and which had resisted capture in 1948, was taken by an Israeli infantry brigade which then moved on to assist in the capture of Ramallah. Elsewhere in the Samarian sector, the key towns of Nablus and Jenin were captured toward the end of the week, following a number of heavy engagements which the Israelis won only thanks to their air superiority. Even though the Jordanian Patton tanks were inferior to the Israeli

the Old City through the Dung Gate. This meant that Old Jerusalem, including the Wailing Wall so dear to Jewish tradition, was in Jewish hands once more.

The same day Ben-Ari's armor, after capturing Ramallah, pushed east and the next day captured Jericho, where the Jordanian resistance was slight; the city was so full of Jordanian troops and armor waiting their turn to approach the Allenby Bridge, giving access to the East Bank and therefore the possibility of regrouping, that it was impossible to organize a defensive posture at short notice. Some Israeli armor actually crossed the Jordan bridges, although there was no serious intention of

BELOW: *Israeli troops celebrate their capture of the Wailing Wall in the Old City of Jerusalem, which fell on 7 June.*

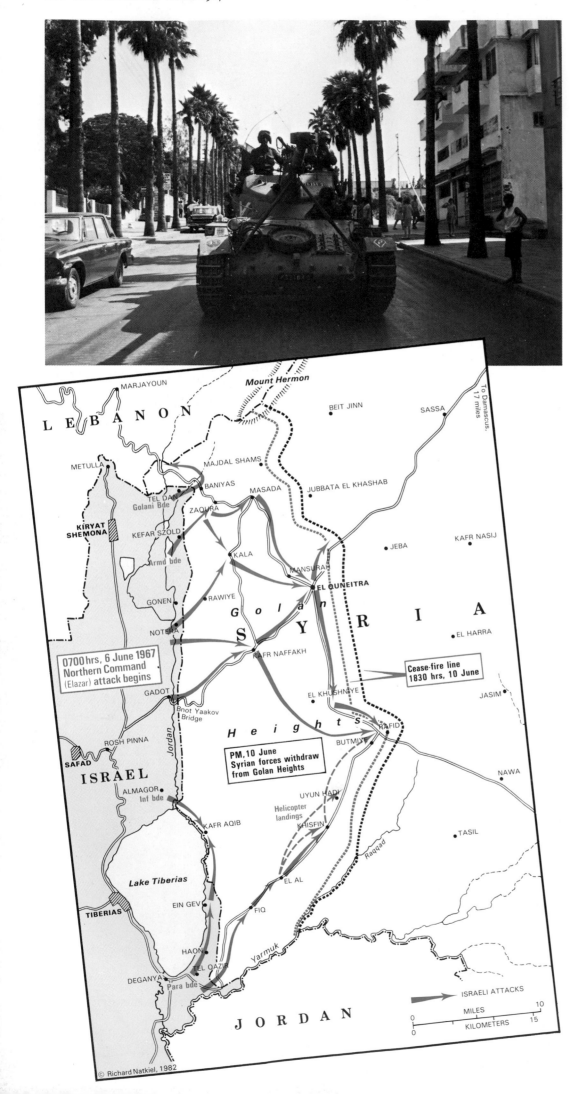

moving on to Amman; Israeli interest was in the West Bank, and no further. Meanwhile the Jerusalem Brigade moved south from Jerusalem and took Bethlehem and Hebron without trouble, for the Arab Legion had already withdrawn from these centers. By this time all the Jordanian forces were across the river, apart from a few isolated units, and the West Bank was in Israeli hands. Chaim Herzog, a brigadier who was subsequently to write the most detailed account of the Arab-Israeli wars, was appointed military governor of this newly acquired territory.

Among the settlements occupied by the Israelis in the West Bank were those known as the Etzion Block, which up to 1947 had been Jewish villages on which much toil and blood had been spent, and which after 1947 had been razed by the Jordanians and re-created as Arab settlements. The emotion which their recapture (and subsequent resurrection as Jewish settlements peopled by the children of the 1947 families) aroused among Israelis was very deep. It symbolized the deep feelings which most Jews had for the territory, and it explains the strength of the subsequent movement to recolonize this territory, thereby creating a 'fact' of Jewish occupation which would make less likely its restitution to the Arabs.

In all, on the Central Front Israel lost about 550 dead, and 2500 of its troops were wounded. Largely because of their vulnerability to air attack, the Jordanian losses were much heavier, probably amounting to 6000 in dead and prisoners. Thousands of Arabs living in the West Bank accompanied the Jordanian Army in its retreat to the East Bank, and many more followed when the Israeli occupation was seen to be a long-term affair. This exacerbated the Palestinian refugee problem, a problem which Israelis still vainly hoped would disappear of its own accord.

On the Northern Front, facing Syria, it was the Israeli command's hope that heavy fighting would be postponed. This was because Syria was very much a Soviet protégé, and Russian intervention, though not considered likely, was something to be avoided at all costs. Secondly, with its hands full in Sinai, Israel simply could not spare forces for a full-scale war against the Syrians, at least not for the first few days. Syria's activity in the first days of the war corresponded so closely to the Israeli desires that subsequently some Egyptians and Jordanians (including King Hussein) could talk about a 'betrayal' by Damascus. True, the Syrian government issued highly aggressive declarations and stirring com-

TOP LEFT: *An Israeli AMX-13 tank passes through Tiberias en route to Syria.*
LEFT: *A map illustrating Israeli operations against Syria.*
RIGHT: *Israeli paratroopers view the Wailing Wall after Jerusalem fell.*

muniques about the successes of its armed forces, but actual activity was at a very low level. The severe damage wrought on the Syrian Air Force after it had attacked Haifa on the first day of the war was one inducement to a quiet campaign, but habitual Syrian caution and reluctance to move from words to deeds was probably the main factor. Syrian guns did bombard Israeli forces, but ground fighting was confined to a few reconnaissances which were terminated as soon as stiff resistance was encountered. Despite previous pro-

LEFT: *The difficult terrain of the Golan Heights hampered the advance of Israeli forces into Syria.*
BELOW: *Israeli armored personnel carriers advance on the Golan Heights. Israel's Northern Command was outnumbered.*

mises, Syrian troops were not sent to help Jordan during this war.

The Golan Heights, on which the Syrian artillery was stationed, was a plateau ranging from 500–9000 feet in height, sufficient to give the gunners a great advantage in range and target-finding. The plateau is about 45 miles long, stretching south from Mount Hermon. The drop toward the Israeli lowlands is very steep, making it a natural frontier which is difficult to assault. Having occupied the Heights for almost 20 years, the Syrian Army had considerably fortified them, and these fortifications stretched back in depth to protect the few highways leading toward Damascus. In summer 1967 the

bulk of the Syrian Army was deployed here, especially around the town of Kuneitra. It was near Kuneitra that the striking force of the army was located, consisting of two armored and two mechanized brigades. Additional armor, in the form of armored battalions, was attached to each of the infantry brigades that were in position nearer the frontier. Israel's Northern Command, headed by David Elazar, was somewhat weaker than the opposing Syrians, consisting of three armored and five infantry brigades; moreover, some of Elazar's forces were sent to help the campaign against Jordan by attacking and capturing Jenin.

Because of the intensity of the Syrian

bombardment, the Israeli staff was under considerable popular pressure to attack the Golan Heights immediately, but it was not until 9 June that a serious offensive was launched. This was directed toward the north, the object being to gain the use of the road passing through Banias and leading toward Kuneitra. The escarpment here was very steep, and for this reason the Syrians had deployed fewer guns than in the easier terrain of the south. The key defensive position for this advance was Tel Faher, whose capture would permit the Israelis to attack an even stronger fortified area, Tel Azaziat, from the rear. The 'Golani' Brigade was entrusted with the Tel Faher attack, which consisted of a

sequence of assaults on successive Syrian positions. Minefields, wire obstacles, intensive trench systems, gun and machine-gun positions behind concrete all had to be taken in hand-to-hand fighting that sometimes resulted in positions being captured and then held by just one or two Israeli soldiers who had escaped serious injury. By evening on 9 June Tel Faher was in Israeli hands and the Golani Brigade moved toward Tel Azaziat. With the advantage of attacking from an unexpected direction, and having a few tanks as stiffening, the Brigade captured that position soon after dark. Meanwhile, an almost equally desperate struggle was being fought by Albert Mandler's armored brigade as it climbed upward to Na'mush and Q'ala. Led by bulldozers to find and clear a way, the tanks overcame successive Syrian positions, but only with considerable loss; it was the bulldozers and their unprotected crews which suffered most.

In general, in the northern part of the Golan Heights, the Israelis had captured the first ridge by the end of 9 June. Further south, Israeli infantry, in less intensive operations, advanced from Mishmar Hayarden, crossed the Jordan, and

RIGHT: *Israel's Prime Minister, Levi Eshkol, visits army reservists on 14 June. Menachem Begin stands behind him on the left.*
BELOW: *Jubilant Israeli troops pull back from the Syrian front for a rest period.*

LEFT: *Israeli M50 Super Sherman tanks advance past a disabled AMX-13 on the Syrian front.*

captured sufficient positions to clear a route for reinforcements to pass from the Central Front, where operations against Jordan were virtually complete. Soon Uri Ram's and Bar-Kochva's armored brigades arrived from the West Bank. By 10 June Kuneitra appeared to be threatened from two directions, from Mansoura by the Golani Brigade and Bar-Kochva's armor, and from Wassett by Mandler's Brigade. With this, and the intensive Israeli air attacks (which were more intense than any the Egyptians had suffered), the Syrians began to lose their nerve. Strong defensive positions were demolished by their withdrawing defenders, and in places retreat developed more or less spontaneously into rout. Probably because fuel supply had been interrupted by air strikes, many Syrian tanks were abandoned. When the UN ceasefire entered into effect at 1830 on 10 June, the Israelis were in clear control of the Golan Heights, having occupied Kuneitra and Mount Hermon. The ceasefire line represented a reverse of the previous situation; now it was the Israeli troops who could look down on the Syrian lowlands, the Plain of Damascus.

It is indicative of Israel's strong diplomatic position that the ceasefire, in effect, was timed to come into force at a moment convenient to it rather than to its enemies. The Arab side had been considerably weakened by the refusal of the USSR to supply replacement weapons so long as the war continued. Moscow had not wanted this war, wanted it to end as soon as possible, and did not feel inclined to offer more support than was necessary to the Arab governments who had been foolish enough to provoke a war. On the other hand, the Russians wished to maintain their influence in the Middle East, and every military reverse suffered by Egypt and Syria seemed to show the risks of relying on Soviet friendship and Soviet weapons. At the UN, the USSR representative pressed for a ceasefire as soon as Egypt had indicated that a ceasefire would be acceptable. But when Syria announced her acceptance of the ceasefire on 9 June the Israelis had not yet reached the positions they intended to occupy, and they pressed on despite the ceasefire bid. At this point the Russians became uneasy, and began to hint that should a ceasefire fail to materialize the Soviet Union would have to consider intervening more actively. Increased Soviet participation was something which the USA did not relish, and this may have been a factor in inducing Israel finally to accept the ceasefire. Much more important, however, was the circumstance that by dusk on 10 June Israel had got what it wanted.

CONFRONTATION AND ATTRITION

Not for the first time in modern history, crushing defeat brought a salutary shock to the defeated, and an unhealthy complacency, if not arrogance, to the victorious. The 1967 war, which seemed to show the unquestionable superiority of the Israeli Defense Forces over the Arab forces, in fact resulted in such an improvement in the quality of the Arab forces that the balance of power and influence in the region began to move against Israel. However, it was not until the war of 1973 had been fought that this alarming fact became evident to the Israelis. The fundamental Israeli mistake was the all-too-easy assumption that the 1967 victory had been won by an inherent and inevitable superiority, by an excellence of standards and performance which the Arabs would never be able to match. The truth was that the result of the 1967 war was determined largely by Arab incompetence, not by Israeli excellence. As soon as Nasser, at long last, realized that there was something fundamentally wrong with his forces, the qualitative gap between the Israeli and Egyptian forces began to narrow.

The most important factor in the renaissance of the Arab armed forces was the USSR, for whom the Six Day War had been an unpleasant experience that had seemed to threaten hard-won Soviet influence in the Middle East. But apart from restocking and retraining the armed forces of the so-called progressive Arab states, Moscow attempted to win every attainable advantage for its friends at the diplomatic level. Actual success here was meager, but at least the Soviet efforts did something to restore Moscow's reputation in the region. At the United Nations the Soviet delegation was foremost in demanding that Israel return to the pre-1967 frontiers. This was something that Israel would not do, at least without guarantees of Israel's own specification. Since such guarantees were virtually unobtainable, it would not be unfair to describe Israel's attitude as 'what we have we hold.' Having in 1967 created new frontiers which were actually defensible, like the Golan Heights and the water barrier provided by the Suez Canal and the Gulf of Suez, Israel was not going to return to a pre-1967 situation. Because the 1967 war had been so obviously provoked by Nasser, there was considerable sympathy for the Israeli position in the UN during and immediately after the 1967 war. The USSR found it impossible to get a vote of condemnation passed against Israel, and henceforth contented itself with repeated efforts to get the 1967 frontiers restored, an ambition which it

RIGHT: *The shell of an Egyptian T-34/85 tank, knocked out during the Six Day War, sinks into the sands of the Sinai, 1971.*
PREVIOUS PAGES: *Flames and smoke pour from Egyptian refineries after being hit by Israeli guns in an artillery duel, 1968.*

ABOVE: *Israel's Foreign Minister Abba Eban (left) and General Gavish (center) set out to inspect army units, 1967.*
LEFT: *Refugees leave Israeli-occupied territory for Jordan, across the makeshift spans of the wrecked Allenby Bridge.*

habitually termed 'the elimination of the consequences of Israeli aggression.' It might be noted, however, that the USSR never departed from its 1948 position of accepting the existence of Israel as a state, despite the occasions when a call for the destruction of Israel would have won it many new friends in the Middle East.

Mutual recrimination after the war was not allowed to disturb the essential relationships between the USSR and friendly Arab governments. The latter might resent the USSR's refusal to supply arms during that conflict, and not hide their feeling that in many respects Soviet weapons had proved inferior to the Western weapons used by Israel. The Russians made little secret, in private, of their feeling that Nasser had made an ass of himself, and that the Syrians and Egyptians had been incapable of making good and proper use of the Soviet weaponry. Implicitly, perhaps, both parties recog-

nized that their partner's view had some validity. In the following years the USSR would go much further than it had previously dared in supplying really late-model weapons, and in sending Soviet military personnel to the Middle East. For his part Nasser, realizing that his armed services needed a radical shake-up, accepted the Soviet premise that what was wrong was the class structure of his forces. The elimination of the old officer class and the granting of commissions to capable men from fairly humble class backgrounds did in fact contribute to the later effectiveness of the Egyptian forces. This was partly because the relationship between officers and men became closer (although never as close as in the Israeli Army) and partly because this enabled a new reservoir of talent to be tapped; the vast majority of the population had never been properly utilized for Egypt's armed forces because an apparent inadequacy of competent officers limited the overall size.

A first step, itself good for the morale of the country and for Nasser's reputation, was the court-martialling of officers responsible for, or conveniently said to be responsible for, the 1967 defeats. It was at this time that Field Marshal Amer de-

cided that suicide was the best way out. He was succeeded as C-in-C by Mohammed Fawzi, an uncorrupt if unimaginative man who had the reputation of an ultra-strict disciplinarian. Nasser realized that Fawzi was not the man to lead the army to victory, but was just what was required to pull the Army together. As Chief of Staff, Nasser chose Abdal Riadh, an intellectual and sociable character driven by the belief that the Egyptian Army must, sooner rather than later, take its revenge on Israel. Riadh was a man of great competence and flexibility (he even got on well with the Russian General Zakharov, which was not easy) and his almost accidental death during an exchange of fire over the Suez Canal in 1969 was a very serious loss.

Other officers of similar social background and training to Fawzi and Riadh lost their jobs. Often they were graduates of West Point or Sandhurst who, in the 1960s, had attended military academies in the USSR and there acquired a distaste for the Soviet way of doing things. Obviously, with Nasser pressing Moscow for an ever more intimate military relationship, that attitude alone was enough to justify their dismissal.

Immediately the Six Day War was over

a Soviet delegation, led by the Soviet President Podgorny, arrived in Cairo to help solve the immediate problems. The USSR, apparently, made no difficulties about the replacement of Egyptian equipment losses. But Nasser wanted more than this, and so did his successor, Sadat. The background of Soviet-Arab relationships in the period between the 1967 and 1973 wars is the constant struggle, eventually successful for the most part, of Egyptian leaders, envoys and delegations, to extract from Moscow more military assistance than Moscow was really willing to give. The way in which the Egyptians played upon the Soviet fear of losing influence in the Middle East was probably as skillful as the Israelis' exploitation of the obsessive

RIGHT: *An Israeli Army patrol drives along a dirt track bordering the Suez Canal in November 1969.*

ABOVE: *In September 1969 the IDF Air Force took delivery of its first McDonnell Douglas F-4E Phantom fighter/attack aircraft from the United States. In October they attacked SAM sites.*
LEFT: *Israeli soldiers watch the oil storage tanks of Suez burning after a two-day artillery duel across the Canal in 1969.*

US fear of communism in extracting weapons from their patrons. All this was achieved at a time when American presidents and the Soviet leadership were working for *détente*, with both superpowers eager to improve their relationships. For both the Egyptian and Israeli governments, such a *détente* was unwelcome but manageable.

Accompanying Podgorny was the Soviet General Zakharov, a somewhat coarse character who had the reputation of getting things done. By this time Nasser was convinced that the best way of shaking up the Egyptian forces would be to obtain the help of outside experts, namely the Russians. So General Zakharov did not go home. He was given a civilian suit and a black beret (presumably to conceal his presence from unfriendly Egyptians rather than from the west, whose intelligence services would hardly have missed this important development), and put in charge of the Soviet reconstruction of the Egyptian forces. A natural bully, he was possibly an ideal person for this job, and he was certainly not going to approve of great arms shipments from the USSR until he was convinced that the Egyptians were fit to use them.

Soon, probably persuaded both by Nasser and Zakharov, Moscow agreed to go further than it had ever gone with a non-communist ally, and dispatched not the hundred or so training advisers originally envisaged, but many more than that, to enable Soviet personnel to work at brigade level, and then at battalion level.

The quality of these advisers varied, and so did their reception by the Egyptian officers. When it became clear that in technical disputes the Soviet advisers would have the last word there was a natural feeling of resentment among Egyptian officers, and the arrogance of some of the Russians made this worse. But Nasser knew that without the Russians, Egypt would never create an army capable of taking on Israel, at least in Nasser's own lifetime.

The 1967–73 period was not a period of peace, but a continuation of the 1967 war by other means. The ceasefire lines were observed because there seemed no alternative, but the Arab states made it clear that they would never be accepted as permanent. From time to time peace settlements were suggested, and for a few weeks one mediator or another would flit between Egypt, Syria, Israel and the USA, but no results were forthcoming. The UN did eventually pass its Resolution 242, which recommended the withdrawal of Israel's forces from the recently occupied areas in exchange for a declaration by all the states of the area guaranteeing secure and recognized boundaries 'free from threats or acts of force.' The last provision implied the acceptance of a permanent Israel. Egypt and Jordan, as well as Israel, accepted the Resolution, but subsequently could not agree on its interpretation. But it remained in force as a guideline for an eventual peace.

The intensity of the armed struggle, which continued on a scale less than all-out war, differed from year to year and from week to week. An early intensification beyond desultory gunfire was the sinking of the Israeli destroyer *Eilat* in October 1967. In September, in retaliation for heavy Egyptian shelling of Israeli ships in the Gulf of Suez, Israeli artillery had bombarded Egyptian cities within reach along the Suez Canal. Suez, Kantara, and Ismailia were the main victims, suffering many casualties, mainly of civilians attempting to lead their normal lives. Eventually the populations realized that their home towns had become uninhabitable, and took to the road as refugees. In October, an Israeli flotilla led by the *Eilat* (formerly the British *Zealous* of late World War II vintage) was patrolling this troubled region and when about fifteen miles north of Port Said was attacked by Soviet-built missile gunboats of the *Komar* series. These boats were still in Port Said harbor, and had therefore not been noted on the Israeli radar. A first *Styx* missile struck the *Eilat* in the area of the boiler-room and a few minutes later another arrived, causing further damage. Two hours later, just as Israeli rescue operations seemed likely to be successful, a third missile struck, set off ammunition, and the *Eilat* went down. There were 47 dead and 90 wounded.

This success was a boost for Nasser's reputation and for Arab morale in general, being the first decisive success over Israel since the end of the war. It was also a boost for Soviet influence, putting an end to rumors that Soviet weapon technology was backward. For most of the world's navies, including the US and British, it came as something of a shock for it not only announced the true beginning of the missile age in naval warfare, but it was accompanied by a realization that the Red

ABOVE: *A soldier mans his observation post overlooking the Suez Canal at Kantara during the War of Attrition in 1970.*
ABOVE LEFT: *An Israeli Army jeep passes through the eastern part of Kantara on the Suez Canal in July 1969. Continual skirmishing along the Canal eventually made the town uninhabitable.*
RIGHT: *Israeli artillerymen prepare to move off with their 155mm self-propelled howitzer in the Canal area, 1969.*

Navy had developed surface-to-surface missile ships further than had other navies.

As the Egyptians expected from past experience, Israeli retribution was not long in coming. It took the form of an unprecedently heavy bombardment, directed not against targets near Port Said, but at the other end of the Canal, where Egypt had a petrochemical complex. Refineries and chemical plants around Suez burned for days, causing an enormous financial loss and economic damage. Possibly the scale of this Israeli response explains why during the following year hostilities took the form of only light and sporadic exchanges of fire. Another factor was that Russian ships in Egyptian ports, which hitherto had gone to sea when any attack was expected, began to stay in these ports, making it likely that an Israeli bombardment would result in Soviet losses, a likelihood that the Israelis presumably treated as a serious risk.

In this period Israel's comparative neglect of artillery in preference to ground support aircraft meant that it was at a disadvantage in artillery duels across the Canal, and this is one reason for the wider ranging Israeli retributive actions. The

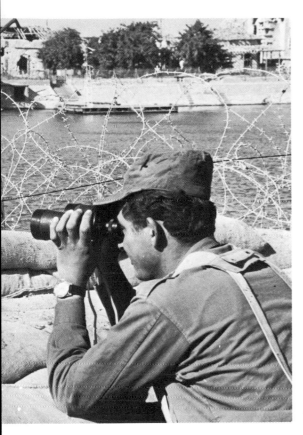

His air force was still not in a condition to win even local air superiority and, as a result, Israeli reprisals in the early months of the war of attrition were heavy. By the end of 1969 Egyptian surface-to-air missile launchers in the Canal area had been destroyed and few Egyptian interceptors managed to interfere with the Israeli aerial pounding of Egyptian troops. Other Israeli responses in the summer and fall of 1969 included commando raids on targets in the Nile Valley; unnerving Israeli reconnaissance flights over Cairo itself, followed by bomb attacks on targets progressively nearer to Cairo; an Israeli armored raid some 50 miles into Egypt; and a seaborne landing to capture and remove an Egyptian radar installation. All Nasser could do was blame the Americans, who in September had begun to deliver Phantom aircraft to Israel.

In January 1970 Israeli bombing was extended to the urban populations of the Nile Valley. Moshe Dayan, who had retained his portfolio as Minister of Defense, rather overexultantly announced that all Egypt would be regarded as the battlefield in the war of attrition. Nasser, aware both that the Egyptians were in a

highly vulnerable situation and that this alarming vulnerability gave him new arguments to use with the Russians, hurried to Moscow. In a series of dramatic negotiations, which took the nature sometimes almost of confrontations, Nasser obtained much of what he wanted from his reluctant hosts. He did not get the MiG-25 interceptors that he felt he needed to counter the Israeli Phantoms, but he did induce the Russians to take a number of unprecedented steps. First he persuaded them to let him have SAM-3 missile launchers, which were effective against low-flying aircraft (the SAM-2, which had failed so miserably in the Six Day War, had since been improved, but was still inferior at low altitudes). Not only this, but faced with the impossibility of training Egyptian troops to handle these missiles in the short time he allowed himself, he obtained the loan of Soviet Red Army personnel to operate them in Egypt.

Moscow had long regarded the dispatch of serving troops into foreign countries, where they might actually become involved in war, as a very risky and undesirable step. It had never done this before, except in countries belonging to the Communist

most spectacular of these, in October 1968, saw commandos transported in French-supplied Sud-321 helicopters for over 200 miles into Egyptian territory, where they attacked Nile bridges and a transformer station 300 miles south of Cairo.

In mid-1969 Nasser proclaimed a 'war of attrition' against Israel. He had just visited Moscow and was confident that the USSR would continue to support his political demands and, while wary of any action which might bring the USA and the USSR into confrontation, would probably respond positively to small-scale Egyptian armed action which demonstrated that the Arab forces had improved. Nasser was also aware of moral pressure being put upon him by the renewal of *Fedayeen* activity across the Jordanian and Syrian ceasefire lines. The demonstrated failure of conventional armed forces in 1967 had made the *Fedayeen* alternative more attractive, and cross-frontier raids had therefore intensified. Nasser's war of attrition was designed to show that the Palestinian guerrillas were not the only people fighting Israel. It was to consist mainly of artillery and commando attacks on the Israeli forces lining the eastern bank of the Suez Canal. Nasser was well aware that Israel was too small to be able to sustain the economic costs of maintaining its army at anywhere near full strength for a long period, yet that is what Israel would be forced to do in order to protect its vastly expanded frontiers from commando-style raids. In any case, by choosing the time and place of each attack, the Egyptians were likely to inflict high casualty rates on their opponents. Nasser had not, however, solved the problem of Israeli air strength.

bloc. Moreover neither Nasser nor the Arabs were regarded as very steady allies, to whom such heavy responsibility could be entrusted. But with the Egyptian air defense in a stage of collapse, a disintegration of the Egyptian regime could already be envisaged; after all, a state which cannot defend its own people does not usually last long. Hence the USSR, in Nasser's argument, could choose between losing a friendly government in Cairo by refusing Egypt's air-defense needs, or risking a clash with the USA by raising its military commitments to Egypt to a new level. In the end, obviously not without some inner anguish, the Kremlin obliged Nasser and thereby preserved its most important bridgehead of influence in the

LEFT: *Burning oil refineries at Port Suez form the backdrop to this Israeli officer's observation of Egyptian military activity.*
BELOW: *An Egyptian sentry, his AK-47 assault rifle at the ready, guards the deserted waterfront at Suez in 1970.*

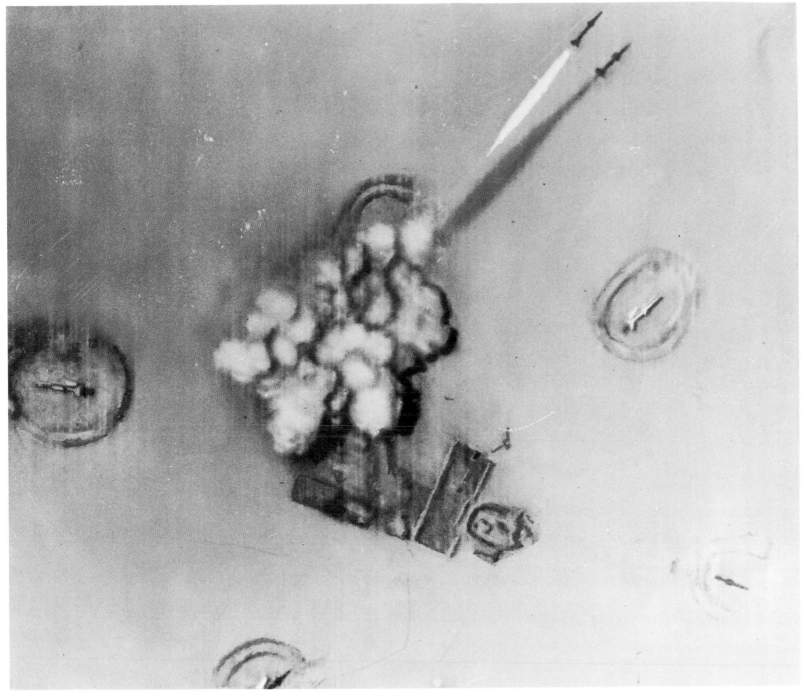

ABOVE: *An Egyptian SA-2 Guideline surface-to-air missile blasts off from its launcher. Six missiles are deployed in protective emplacements around a central launch control complex and the SA-2's Fan Song fire-control radar. This arrangement is typical of Soviet air defense tactics. The photograph was taken by an Israeli strike aircraft in 1970.*

Middle East. At the same time it took the precaution of telling the US President what it was doing, and why. The implication passed to Washington was that if the US was unable to restrain Israel, then the USSR would have to do it, by placing Soviet-manned missile launchers in vulnerable areas of Egypt (excluding, however, areas near the frontier). Cairo, Alexandria, and the Aswan Dam were among the first centers to receive Soviet missiles, and by the end of 1970 about 80

Soviet-manned missile installations had been established, presumably with crews approaching 20,000 men. In addition, to protect the missile sites, the USSR sent to Egypt Red Air Force units amounting to more than one hundred aircraft, located at half a dozen airfields transferred to Soviet control. The decision to send Soviet pilots was accompanied by accusations in the Soviet press that the USA was sending American pilots to Israel.

In February 1970 the Israelis made a destructive attack, probably by accident, on an Egyptian metalworks, resulting in heavy loss of life. This was regarded as an outrage even in the context of the war of attrition, and probably helped to stiffen Soviet resolve and may have been the final push needed to persuade Moscow to send Red Air Force pilots. It also may have been one of the factors raising doubts in Washington about the benefits to the

USA of satisfying further Israeli demands for aircraft (Skyhawks and Phantoms were on the Israeli request list). In April Dayan announced that the deep raids into Egypt would cease. It was made clear to the Russians that should they bring their missiles closer than about 15 miles from the Canal, a new and fraught situation would be created. This was a recommendation which the Russians would follow only so long as it was convenient, for in the face of heavy Israeli air attacks in the summer of 1970 a joint Soviet-Egypt endeavor installed missiles along the Canal. Often, new SAM sites were set up overnight; once set up, they were hard to destroy without risking heavy Israeli aircraft loss.

In July, for the first time, Soviet pilots in MiG-21 fighters intervened in the warfare around the Canal. They chased off a couple of Israeli Skyhawks without,

LEFT: *General Haim Bar-Lev, the architect of Israel's defenses in Sinai, is interviewed by journalists after an operation on Shadwan Island in January 1970.*
BELOW: *Israeli Army signallers pictured during the operation on Shadwan Island.*

it seems, attempting to shoot them down. The Israeli, response, unsurprisingly, was less gentle. At the end of the month, in what appears to have been a carefully planned operation, Soviet MiG-21s were lured into action against Israeli aircraft and were thereby led into an aerial ambush in which four of them were destroyed.

BELOW: *The wreckage of airliners destroyed in an Israeli commando raid on Beirut International Airport in December 1968. The DC-4 (foreground) was one of 13 aircraft destroyed.*

Apparently, Egyptian airmen viewed this discomfiture of the Soviet pilots with a certain satisfaction; having been told by the Russians that it had been them, not their Soviet-supplied aircraft, which had failed in the 1967 war, it was not unpleasurable to see the Soviet airmen worsted in the same way.

Having demonstrated their indispensability to the Egyptians, for by this time it was evident that Israel was losing its once-absolute air superiority, the Russians were in a good position to persuade Nasser to moderate his ambitions. Instead

of insisting on an immediate return to the 1967 frontiers, Nasser was willing to accept a ceasefire once Israeli air superiority (in effect its military superiority) had been eliminated. In August 1970 therefore the war of attrition came to an end, with both Israel and Egypt accepting a ceasefire. Nasser presumably had been encouraged by Soviet assurances that its provisions could be advantageously violated, for no sooner had it come into effect than Egyptians and Russians installed more missiles parallel to and even closer to the Canal. The range of the newly

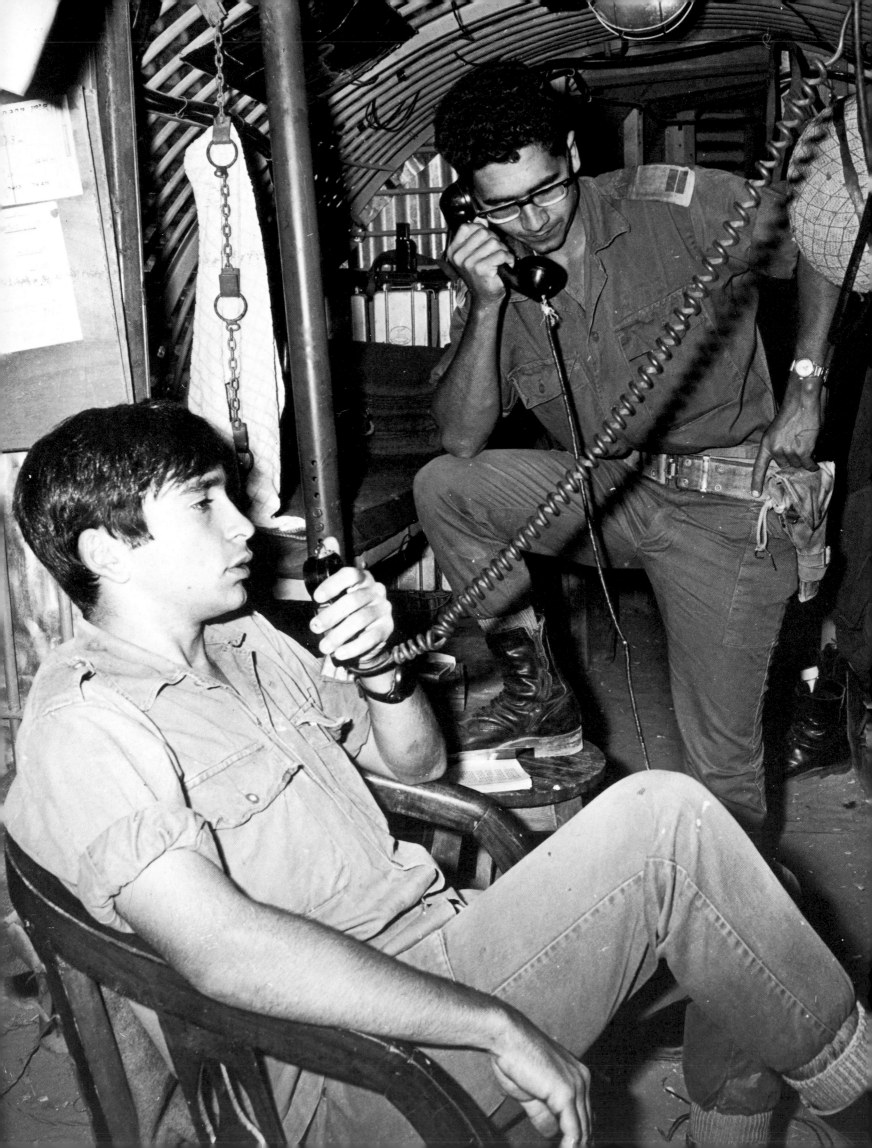

ABOVE: *Israeli soldiers look down on the lighthouse on Shadwan Island during their operation in January 1970.*
LEFT: *Sgt Eli and Lt Avraham man their command bunker in the Israeli Canal defenses – the Bar Lev Line.*

installed SAM-3 missiles now covered the Israeli defenses along the east bank of the Canal to a depth of about 12 miles. Israel protested against these violations but the US government, which at the time was somewhat disenchanted by what seemed to be Israeli intransigence and violence, was not prepared to take forceful action.

Meanwhile, Israel had to find ways of reacting to the new situation. The period after the 1967 war had not quite gone as had been hoped. In the war the Suez Canal had been blocked, and the expected loss of Canal revenue had been expected to moderate the Egyptian posture. However, other Arab countries, led by oil-producing Saudi Arabia, hitherto regarded by Nasser as hostile, began to subsidize Egypt's continuing war preparations. Now, the Israeli defending troops on the east bank of the Canal were being subject to intensive artillery barrages. Early in 1969, a series of fixed fortifications along the Canal, the Bar-Lev Line, was built to

provide shelter for defending Israeli troops. This was the largest civil engineering work ever undertaken by Israel and, more important, it marked a departure from the previous emphasis on mobile warfare. In a sense, it was to play the same role in Israeli military planning as the Maginot Line had once played in French.

Israeli arms procurement was threatened in 1968, when President De Gaulle imposed an arms embargo. Fifty Mirage fighters and five motor gunboats were among the Israeli purchases whose delivery was forbidden by De Gaulle and his successor, Pompidou. After some years the French once more became accommodating, but not before Paris had been humiliated by the escape from Cherbourg of the five Israeli gunboats. This was accomplished on Christmas Eve, 1969, by the Israeli crews who had been sent to bring the boats to Israel on the eve of the ban, and who had remained on board. This escape from a closely guarded harbor was achieved with a good deal of support from Israeli intelligence and from Israeli officers on mission in Paris, as well as from sympathizers among French officials.

The ability to tap great reserves of sympathy in most countries was a great and skillfully exploited advantage for Israel

in its struggle for an assured existence. In the West, the majority of Jews chose not to immigrate to Israel, but nevertheless regarded the new Jewish state with great emotional attachment. From among these people it was possible to recruit active support for Israeli intelligence activities. More important, however, was the spontaneous support that was not sought but could always be relied upon. This was particularly important in the field of public relations. In the conflict between Arab and Jew, the Jewish case was put before the Western public far more effectively than the Arab. Newspapers, and other media, hesitated to present views that might be construed as opposed to Israel. Those that did might find themselves branded as anti-Semitic by Jewish readers. Critical letters from Jewish readers or listeners, taken in total, amounted to a very effective form of post-publication censorship. Alleged prepublication censorship of a patchy, but nevertheless effective, kind may have come from the many activist Jews employed in one or other stage of production in press or broadcasting. The Arabs could not match this, and were further hampered by their clumsy handling of information. Whereas the Israelis had a shrewd understanding of

the Western public and its thought processes, the Arabs did not appreciate that blatant propaganda would not be believed.

While Israel was being forced into an increasingly unfavorable situation on the frontier with Egypt, the campaign against PLO guerrillas saw some success in the second half of 1970. After the end of the Six Day War the PLO's military wing, El Fatah, felt that the Israeli occupation of Jordan's West Bank provided an opportunity to operate against Israel while remaining within a friendly Arab population. However, Israeli policy in the West Bank was sympathetic toward the Arab population, which did not offer the PLO quite the support and sympathy on which it had counted. There were many actions by the guerrillas, but they were steadily forced out of the West Bank and took refuge in the East Bank, all that now remained of Jordan. Here their actions, often resulting in losses of Israeli civilians, soon brought retribution which was felt not so much by the PLO as by the unwilling host population. After an Israeli school bus had been blown up, a particularly heavy retribution was carried out

in Jordan, ostensibly aimed at the PLO center near Karameh. This took place on 21 March 1968, and tanks and aircraft were included in the Israeli forces. The Jordanian Army, which was inevitably caught up, suffered about 40 fatalities, civilians and PLO a possible 200, while Israeli casualties included 28 dead. The PLO responded by moving further to the east, where they dispersed among the mountains but continued to arrange rocket and artillery fire across the frontiers.

The retribution that their activities brought aroused considerable resentment in Jordan, and in September 1970 King Hussein at last felt strong enough to tackle them. Whereas in Egypt, Syria and Iraq the governments had severely restricted the activities of the *Fedayeen*, even while supporting them with slogans and exhortation, in Jordan the several guerrilla movements operating under the loose auspices of the PLO represented a challenge to the government. The largest group, Al Fatah, exhibited its armed strength in public, organizing roadblocks as well as search-and-seize operations among the general public. It was numerous and strong enough

ABOVE: *Villagers carry out rescue work after an Israeli air raid on Kafar Assad in Jordan.*

to become virtually a state within a state, with King Hussein uneasily aware that any attempt to quell it might lead to a civil war. The Jordanian Army disliked the guerrillas, and in June 1970 clashes developed into heavy fighting in Amman, with about 400 fatalities. Hussein took personal command of his army but the eventual ceasefire between the two sides, signed by Hussein and by Yasser Arafat for the PLO, certainly did not mark a victory for the King, for he had to agree to the dismissal of two generals.

When in September foreign airliners were hijacked to Jordan, tension mounted again. This time Hussein decided to settle the issue once and for all. He authorized his army to regard the new campaign against the guerrillas as a full-scale campaign. In this month, 'Black September,' PLO villages were destroyed, and Bedouin soldiers showed no pity toward the guerrillas. The Syrian government sent a column of tanks into Jordan to help the guerrillas but, without air support, this fell victim to Hussein's tanks and his newly rebuilt air force; the Syrians lost about 100 tanks before they recrossed the frontier. Further Syrian intervention was discouraged by, among other things, the movement of the US Sixth Fleet into the eastern Mediterranean; the US government was unwilling to allow Syria, with its Soviet associations, to overthrow the pro-Western government of Jordan. By the end of the year, having sustained thousands of casualties, the guerrillas were shattered. There was a new agreement, but sporadic fighting continued into 1971 and by the summer of that year the surviving PLO forces had retreated into Syria, where they were retrained and reorganized before being sent on into Lebanon. Here they established their headquarters at Beirut and engaged in raids into northern

BELOW: *During the War of Attrition Israel had to deal with the attacks of Palestinian guerrilla forces. The irregular troops pictured belong to the Palestinian Action Organization and were photographed in October 1969. They are armed with Kalashnikov AK-47 assault rifles supplied by the Soviet Union.*

Israel. They were still under Syrian influence but Syria, as previously, could ensure that the disruptive effect of their presence and of the Israeli retribution they attracted would be felt not in Syria, but in neighboring territory.

Partly because of the strain caused by his mediation of the Jordan crisis, in September 1970 Nasser had died of a heart attack. He had been ill for some years with diabetes, and had been under treatment by Soviet doctors. The latter do not appear to have regarded his condition as dangerous, but probably did not realize that their advice concerning rest and stress was largely ignored by the President. His lieutenant, Anwar Sadat, took over his position, first on a provisional, and then on a constitutionally-approved permanent basis. Because he followed so charismatic and flamboyant a predecessor, Sadat tended to be underestimated, but in perspective he seems to have been a considerably more remarkable man than Nasser. In an age when intelligence services, electronics and media activity had developed to a degree which made surprise hard to achieve, Sadat surprised the world on no fewer than three occasions: by expelling his Soviet advisers in 1972; by launching a

completely unanticipated offensive war against Israel in 1973; and by flying to the Israeli capital to discuss peace and reconciliation in 1977. Those who describe him as the beneficiary of Nasser's labors do Sadat an injustice.

One of Sadat's achievements was to persuade the USSR to increase yet again its shipments of arms at a time when he was clearly intent on using them to make full-scale war against Israel, which the Soviet government did not welcome, initially at least. While obtaining these arms Sadat was paying scant regard to Soviet interests. He assisted the Sudanese leader Numeiry in the suppression of a communist-led coup in Khartoum, and he dismissed from his cabinet Aly Sabri, and others, who were regarded as particularly warm supporters of the USSR. During the resulting icy relations with Moscow arms shipments usually continued on a reduced scale, and when each crisis faded, warmer relations were helped along by Moscow conceding Egyptian demands for weapons that had hitherto been refused.

In March 1971 Sadat told the Kremlin that he regarded that year as the 'year of decision,' leaving no doubts of his intention. Perhaps it was this realization,

rather than the excuses actually offered, which explained the Soviet government's refusal of Sadat's plea for MiG-25 interceptors. But Moscow sent to Egypt more Red Air Force MiG-21 machines, with pilots, and agreed to prolong the stay of Soviet missile personnel, as well as to supply even more missile installations. However, as a precaution against what Moscow feared might happen as a result of Egyptian hotheadedness, the Soviet missile crews were withdrawn well away from the Canal; by this time Egyptian personnel had been trained to handle the SAM-3. In May 1971 the USSR persuaded Egypt to sign a Treaty of Friendship and Co-operation. Sadat, not under-

BELOW: *A heavily camouflaged guerrilla of the Palestine People's Liberation Front.*

No sooner had the Treaty of Friendship been signed than relations cooled. This was because in July 1971 Egypt assisted in suppressing a pro-communist coup in the Sudan. But within a few months both Moscow and Cairo evidently decided that they still needed each other. A visit by Sadat to Moscow produced an evident reconciliation, cemented by Soviet promises of modern weapons in addition to those already agreed. In December Sadat, alarmed that these weapons did not appear to be forthcoming, requested another hearing in Moscow; despite his plea of urgency, he was not granted this until February. Without the promised equipment, Sadat believed he could not launch his proposed military action, and in January, in a public speech, he actually declared that the fight with Israel would

of Nixon-Brezhnev talks unnerving, so in April he went to Moscow. He announced his arrival with a letter to Brezhnev that warned that the Americans would doubtless produce suggestions for the Middle East which would be against Egypt's interest. Interestingly, Sadat also criticized the new willingness of the USSR to allow Soviet Jews to emigrate to Israel. According to Sadat this concession (which the Russians had undertaken in deference to US requests) simply provided Israel with very useful Soviet-trained technicians who would increase Israeli military power. The meetings Sadat had in Moscow were marked by a certain acridity, if not acidity; at one juncture Soviet Defense Minister Grechko cast doubt on Sadat's will to fight. However, Sadat seems to have got what he wanted – a Soviet commitment to

standing the importance that Moscow attached to such scraps of paper, signed willingly but in a state of bewilderment. He had been careful, however, to avoid granting what the USSR had long been requesting, permanent naval bases in Egypt as opposed to the rights extended to Soviet warships to use Egyptian facilities. A feature of the Treaty, which could not have displeased Sadat, was its clear implication that Soviet weapon supplies were intended to bring about the withdrawal of Israel from territory taken from Egypt in 1967. Possibly this Soviet concession was made in exchange for an Egyptian undertaking, enshrined in the Treaty, to consult Moscow before starting any war.

have to be postponed until the Russians could be pushed a little further. Moscow, however, made it plain that with a Nixon-Brezhnev summit meeting scheduled for May, any military action by Egypt would be unwelcome, and should be postponed until after the Summit. It would seem that Sadat gave an appropriate undertaking, in return for Soviet help with surface-to-surface missiles. These medium-range missiles had hitherto been regarded by Moscow as too dangerous for the Egyptians to be entrusted with, since they gave the latter a capacity to bombard Israeli cities.

Sadat, like other Middle East leaders who benefited more from East-West tension than from *détente*, found the prospect

arrange heavy arms deliveries as soon as the US-Soviet summit was over. The joint communique issued at the end of his visit acknowledged that war (covered by the euphemism 'nonpolitical measures') against Israel was justified by Israel's occupation of Arab lands, and that Soviet-Egyptian military co-operation would be strengthened.

Despite this, Sadat obviously distrusted Moscow at this period. After the US-Soviet summit, despite a report received from Brezhnev about its course, Sadat sent a somewhat blunt series of questions to Brezhnev. By far the bluntest was an enquiry about precisely when the new weapons, so often requested by Egypt and so often promised by Moscow, would actually arrive. He waited several weeks for a reply which, when it came, contained little more than platitudes about Soviet-Egyptian friendship. Sadat responded by ordering all Soviet military advisers to leave Egypt within 10 days, all Soviet military installations (mainly missile sites) to be handed over to Egypt, and all Soviet-controlled equipment (for example, Red Air Force aircraft) to be sold to Egypt or removed.

How far short-term fury and longer-term irritation affected this decision is unclear. At the time this 'expulsion' of the USSR from Egypt was regarded in the outside world as a turning point, which in a sense it was. However, perhaps because Sadat's temper cooled, it turned out to be less drastic than it first appeared. Sadat really could not cut himself off from Soviet help at this stag without ruining Egyptian war potential. President Assad of Syria was one of those who realized this, and sent temporizing messages to the Egyptian President. In the end, not all the Soviet advisers left, military academy instructors and weapon-training instructors being retained, and the Red Navy continued to enjoy the use of Egyptian bases. The Russians continued to supply spare parts for Soviet-built equipment. As its effort in Egypt declined, the USSR transferred its interest to Syria, where the army and air force began to benefit from an infusion of Soviet hardware and experience.

Despite Sadat's hard line, the USSR still declined to supply the ultramodern weapons which he had been demanding, and the reconciliation between Sadat and Moscow in early 1973 seems to have been reached not so much by Soviet concessions, as by Sadat's agreeing to limit his proposed military action to the objectives favored by the USSR. Whereas a new war aimed at throwing Israel's frontier back to the 1967 situation might well have brought complications with the USA and was therefore unacceptable, a war intended simply as a way of shocking Israel into a less intransigent posture was acceptable, just acceptable, to Moscow. On this understanding, it seems, Moscow became genuinely more forthcoming with arms supply. Shipments increased in 1973 and among the new weapons supplied was a batch of *Scud* surface-to-surface missiles that could hit Israeli cities from Egyptian launching sites. Not enough of these were supplied to make possible the destruction of Israeli towns, but there were enough to deter the Israelis, through fear of retaliation, from bombing Egyptian cities. It was this new ability to protect Cairo, the Aswan Dam and other centers from bombing attack that was the final prerequisite for Sadat's long-planned war against Israel.

ABOVE RIGHT: *A Palestinian refugee camp.*
RIGHT: *Palestinian guerrillas man the defenses of the town of Irbid in Jordan.*

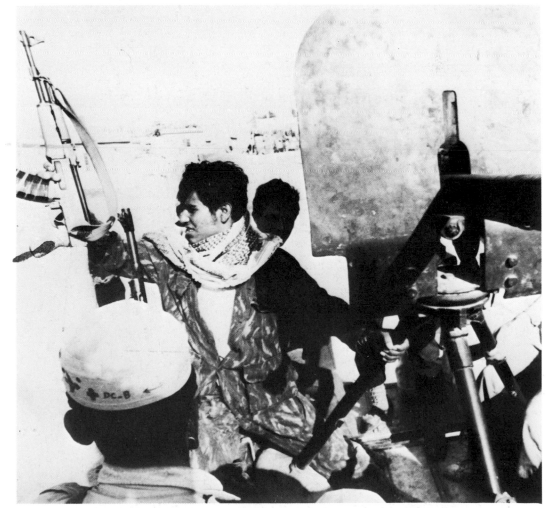

BELOW: *An Israeli M-48 tank moves east across the Suez Canal, 1974.*

THE OCTOBER WAR
—1973—

Although it is legitimate to trace the origin of the 1973 October War to Nasser's decision to reconstruct his forces with the aim of eventually having another go at Israel, it was really Sadat's war. It was Sadat who ensured that the necessary weapons were available, that the detailed planning was started in good time, and it was he who approved and to some extent originated the plans. The timing was his, and so was the realization, with some Soviet prompting, that the aim of the war should be to demonstrate that Egypt and the Arabs were much stronger than Israel and the outside world believed them to be. An acceptable settlement would thereby become more likely.

Operation *Badr* resulted from meticulous planning in which, although Soviet advisers played a significant part in the early stages, the Egyptian military staff proved its competence. The decision to go ahead with the operation was apparently taken in August 1973, although the day and the hour were not settled until later. Originally, Colonel Gadaffi's Libya was to participate, and its forces had been incorporated in the plan. But when Sadat indicated that he was not going to regard Israel's return to the 1967 frontiers as the aim of this new war, Gadaffi and his men withdrew. Syria, however, was steadfast in its partnership with Egypt, and this was cemented in January 1973, when the command of the Egyptian and Syrian forces was unified.

Although units from other Arab countries (Jordan, Iraq, Morocco, Saudi Arabia) would participate in the forthcoming war, Syria and Egypt were the only Arab states destined for total war. Syria had benefited, like Egypt, from Soviet supplies, and its army of about 125,000 men was well equipped. Its two armored divisions and its four mechanized divisions had more modern vehicles than in 1967. Although about 200 old T34 tanks still remained, they were outnumbered by about 1000 of the more recent T54 and T55 models, while a few of the even more modern T62 type were also in service. The Iosif Stalin heavy and PT76 light tanks still existed, but not in significant strength. In accordance with Soviet military practice, the Syrian Army was well-supplied with artillery, and still had about 75 SU-100 self-propelled guns. It had about a dozen SAM-2 and SAM-3 surface-to-air missile batteries and some SAM-6 missiles (these were mobile antiaircraft missiles suited to low-altitude use). *Snapper* and *Sagger* antitank guided weapons were also available. The Syrian Air Force still had a few IL-28 light bombers, but its main strength was about

TOP RIGHT: *The US supplied Israel with A-4H Skyhawks in 1968.*
CENTER RIGHT: *A Mirage III marked with eight victories scored over the EAF.*
RIGHT: *A Shafrir missile on a Mirage III.*

200 MiG-21 interceptors, about 80 MiG-17 and perhaps 30 SU-7 fighter-bombers.

Egypt had more than double Syria's potential, although the weapon models were almost identical. In artillery it had about 1600 medium and heavy guns, with about 150 self-propelled guns. Its tank inventory of about 2000 units included some 100 T62 models, but was dominated by about 1600 T54 and T55 models. A particularly important Soviet export to Egypt was amphibious landing equipment, and also a stock of components for the PMP portable-bridge system. Antiaircraft missiles of the SAM-2 and SAM-3 series amounted to over 700 launchers, and these were supplemented and protected by many

ABOVE: *An Egyptian SA-2 Guideline pictured in its emplacement on the west bank of the Suez Canal in October 1973.*
TOP: *Lockheed C-130 Hercules tactical transport aircraft took part in the Yom Kippur War and the Entebbe Raid in 1976.*

low-level SAM-6 installations. The Egyptians also had SAM-7 antiaircraft missiles, but these low-level portable defense weapons suffered from a small and sometimes ineffective provision of explosive. The numerous antitank missiles, which were to prove so useful in the hands of Egyptian infantry, were of the Soviet *Snapper* and *Sagger* types. Larger surface-to-surface missiles included some 30 medium-range *Scuds* and some 100 *Samlets* for coast defense. *Frog* missiles had also been delivered by the USSR, but their small warheads meant that they had a minor role. The main strength of the Air Force lay in its 200 or so MiG-21 interceptors and its 200 MiG-17 and SU-7 fighter-bombers. These were supplemented by some 40 Mirage IIIs, obtained when France was passing through a pro-Arab period. The medium bomber force, which Moscow still did not want to build up to an extent

that would tempt the Egyptians into heavy raids on Israeli cities, amounted to some 20 TU-16 aircraft; Egyptian requests for the much more effective TU-22 had been repeatedly refused.

Total strength of the Egyptian armed forces was about 323,000 and that of Syria about 137,000. Against this combined figure of 460,000 men, Israel could muster about 400,000, once its 254,000 reservists reached their units. Against the combined Syrian and Egyptian total of about 3500 tanks, Israel could muster some 2000. These were of varying design and vintage. Centurions and US-built Patton tanks were the mainstay of the 10 armored brigades but other types, including sundry captured tanks of Soviet construction, and Super Shermans, were also available. However, it should be noted that although the Israelis were numerically inferior in tanks, their total of about 6000 armored personnel carriers considerably exceeded the Egyptian/Syrian total. This meant that the Israelis still retained a considerable ability to outmaneuver their opponents by swift movements of infantry. Their antitank missiles were of good quality, consisting of optically-tracked

and wire-guided systems originating in the USA (Dragon and TOW) and West Germany (Cobra). But Israel was weak in artillery, and lagging in the antiaircraft missile systems represented by its enemies' SAM variants; the experience of 1967 had strengthened the Israeli belief that aircraft could do a better job than guns or land-based missiles. The Israeli command disposed of about 450 combat aircraft compared to an Egyptian total of 500 and Syrian 300. The Israelis were probably right in their belief that, type for type and man for man, they had a definite qualitative superiority in the air. By this time the USA had replaced France as the principal source of aircraft, although a few score Mirage III, Ouragan, Mystère IV fighter-bombers and Vautour light bombers were still in frontline service. The main striking force consisted of some 150 Phantom fighter-bomber/interceptors and about 180 Skyhawk fighter-bombers. Like its enemies, Israel also had a number of transport aircraft and was numerically superior in helicopters.

The choice of the Jewish Day of Atonement, Yom Kippur, as the start of this war was largely coincidental, and did not greatly benefit the attackers. It was simply that, once the decision to attack had been taken in August, the settlement of final details, together with the need for a countdown period, virtually dictated that the attack would begin toward the end of the first week of October. 6 October was a day when the tides in the Canal were suitable for the first phase of the operation. To attack on the most sacred day in the Jewish calendar did ensure that, because of special leave, the Israeli defensive positions would be undermanned. On the other hand, it helped Israeli publicists to portray the Arab attackers as unfeeling and sacrilegious, and it also helped the Israeli mobilization; with almost all reservists at home that weekend, mobilization notices reached their addresses unusually promptly.

The time for the attack was settled after a good deal of discussion. The Syrians wanted to attack at dawn, when the rising

LEFT: *President Anwar Sadat of Egypt came to power on Nasser's death in September 1970.*
INSET LEFT: *Golda Meir, Israel's Prime Minister during the Yom Kippur War.*
RIGHT: *Egypt's initial offensive 6–8 October 1973.*

*On 6 Oct Resheff's Bde was stretched from Ketuba in the north to the Gulf of Suez inc. Dan's Bde

© Richard Natkiel, 1982

sun behind their troops would hinder the Israelis. The Egyptians preferred to wait for the afternoon, when the most delicate part of their operation, crossing the Canal, could take place with the sun behind them. Having been trained for night fighting, they would still have time to press on with bridging and movement of armor. Suggestions that the Syrians should begin at dawn and the Egyptians later were rejected by the Syrians as it would mean they would fight alone for some hours. The following Egyptian offer to cross the Canal in the afternoon, with the Syrians attacking the following dawn, was dismissed on the grounds that the Syrians would then be seen to be lagging behind the Egyptians. Finally, President Assad of Syria magnanimously agreed that both attacks might start at 1400 hours.

The military planners had hoped that, with luck, the Israelis would not suspect that an attack was coming until two weeks before it was due. On further thought and with the wish becoming father to the thought (because it became increasingly inconceivable that the operation could succeed if the Israelis had so much preparation time) it was decided to count on just five days' warning; as the Israeli mobilization period was reckoned to need a week this would confer considerable advantage. As things turned out, a combination of thoughtful deception technique, Israeli carelessness, and sheer luck permitted the attackers to enjoy the advantage of surprise up to almost the last minute.

Following World War II patterns, and especially knowledge of what the British Army had done in the North African campaign, an elaborate deception plan was created and acted out, with troops moving by day and then quietly disappearing elsewhere by night. An advantage enjoyed by the Egyptians was a high sand rampart built along the western bank of the Canal. This matched a somewhat similar Israeli erection, and appeared to be for defensive purposes. But with SAM missiles preventing Israeli air observation, this rampart provided a screen behind which Egyptian preparation for the Canal crossing could stealthily proceed.

The Israeli intelligence service, which had extensive and high-quality information sources, received considerable evidence, mainly indirect, of activity behind the western bank of the Canal. This information worried several of the few Israeli officers who were aware of it. But intelligence of developments contrary to what is expected by a high command does

not always cause minds to be changed; leading decision-makers in the Israeli High Command and government had long considered that Egypt was in no condition to start another war, and were therefore inclined to reject intelligence findings which conflicted with this belief. One of these skeptics, it appears, was the newly installed Israeli Director of Military Intelligence, who until the very last moment doubted the imminence of an attack. Israeli decision makers who usually would have been more critical of the reports submitted to them were, by chance, preoccupied with other matters. A train hijack in Austria by *Fedayeen*, resulting in an Austrian decision to close a transit camp for Jewish emigrants from the USSR, was one distraction. Another was that an Israeli air operation in September, which caused considerable Syrian air losses and the appearance of Israeli aircraft over Damasc-

us, had given rise to the expectation of some kind of Arab retribution. Syrian troop movements near the frontier, as well as the Egyptian troop movements taking place under cover of an apparent military exercise, were accordingly regarded as preliminary to an avenging incursion rather than a full-scale war.

While the Egyptians and Syrians were successfully engaged in this grand deception, their media and propaganda specialists were preparing a lesser deceit. It was decided that when the attack was launched it would be presented as a response to an Israeli act of aggression on the Red Sea coast of Egypt. The point of this lie, which was to be served up in the form of special announcements on the radio, is obscure. With Arab populations likely to welcome a clear aggressive Arab attack whether it was provoked or not, and with foreign opinion quite able to see what had really happened, this propaganda effort was pointless. Possibly the Egyptians, still lacking self-confidence in war making, relied on the experience of older powers and concocted this falsehood simply because such deception was fashionable in the 20th century. The concept of the contrived pretext would probably have remained fresh in their minds from 1956.

Many IDF units along the Canal had been reporting signs of interesting and potentially significant Egyptian activity for several days. On 5 October they were aware that: Egyptian tanks in serried ranks were on or near the sand platforms that had been built to enable them to fire over the rampart into Sinai; that there were five infantry divisions in place by the Canal; that almost 200 batteries of artillery had been assembled; and that pontoons and bridging equipment were ready. With all these facts, it was hard for Israeli Military Intelligence to deny that something was imminent; indeed the Chief of Naval Intelligence had, several days previously, decided that war was round the corner, but his opinion had been ignored at General Headquarters. Also on 5 October, families were evacuated from Egypt and Russian Syria, which would not have passed unnoticed by Israeli intelligence. Pos-

sibly this was a factor persuading General Elazar, Israeli Chief of Staff, to obtain from the cabinet permission for the forces to be alerted, with a mobilization of a few key reservists. In the morning of 6 October he asked Dayan, the Defense Minister, for permission to make a pre-emptive attack on Syria, while ordering a general mobilization. Dayan would agree only to a small mobilization, but when Prime Minister Golda Meir was asked to settle the issue she agreed to a mobilization of 100,000 men, while agreeing with Dayan about the pre-emptive attack. In view of these developments it was proposed to call a cabinet meeting at 1400 hours.

In fact, preliminary Egyptian operations began before zero hour on 6 October. One of the most important, undertaken by commandos and frogmen, was the blocking of the pipes that the Israelis had laid to take oil down to the surface of the Canal; setting the Canal on fire was one of the means the Israelis had chosen for preventing a Canal crossing. This operation was undertaken under cover of darkness, with the defenders noticing nothing. Actually, the pipes had been so neglected by the

RIGHT: *An Egyptian Air Force MiG-21 is shot down over the Suez Canal in 1973.*
BELOW: *Israeli reservists report to base.*

Israelis that it is unlikely that they would have functioned in any case. Other, less dramatic, endeavors had removed Egyptian mines from the Canal where they conflicted with the planned movements. The Israelis did notice this, but were confused because as part of their deception plan the Egyptian seamen at the same time laid mines in other parts of the Canal.

On the Sinai front, the real battle began a few minutes after 1400 hours, when the massed Egyptian artillery – guns, mortars and rocket projectors – opened the bombardment. Several hundred Egyptian bombers and fighter-bombers made their contribution a few minutes later. By 1430 1000 rubber boats, mostly carrying eight men each, were grounding on the Israeli shore of the Canal, and from 1500 hours the Israeli fortresses composing the Bar-Lev Line began to fall into the attackers' hands. Soon the Egyptian sappers could use water cannon to wash about 80 gaps through the sand rampart on the Israeli side of the Canal, thereby facilitating the building of bridges and the operation of ferries. By nightfall there were about 80,000 Egyptians occupying freshly dug positions along the Canal, well inside the

BELOW: *Israeli artillerymen fire a captured Katyusha rocket battery on the Canal.*

Bar-Lev Line. Light PT-76 tanks, the first to come across the Canal and pass through the rampart breaches, were in support.

Surprise, innovation, and the general undermanning of the Bar-Lev Line were the explanations for this initial success. Some of the Bar-Lev fortresses were actually unmanned, and most were captured during the first day. Others were overrun later, or were successfully or unsuccessfully evacuated by their defenders while one, at the northern end, never surrendered.

Crossing a defended water barrier, even one of only 75 yards like the Suez Canal, is always a perilous enterprise, and the Egyptian Army had performed this task impeccably; indeed, many of its units had been practicing this operation for the previous three years. The next stage was equally successful and equally well thought out. This was the solution of the problem posed by the anticipated Israeli armored counterattack on the Egyptian positions, which were held by infantrymen because the medium tanks were still on the western bank. At a quite late stage, it was decided to provide the first wave of infantry with unprecedented numbers of hand-held *Sagger* antitank rockets. Originally it had been intended merely that the

infantry should be strong in this weapon, and thoroughly trained both in its use and its particular application on the day of the assault. But so daunting was the threat of the inevitable Israeli armored counterattack that it was finally decided to denude the infantry formations on the west bank of the Canal, which handed over their *Saggers* to the assault infantry. The latter had therefore an extremely high concentration of these weapons. On landing from their dinghies, those soldiers and officers equipped with this weapon immediately set off at a trot for their predetermined defensive line, which was about three miles inside the Bar-Lev Line. A few minutes after they had settled down in these positions they were confronted by the Israeli tanks.

The first Israeli armored movement, in accordance with a long-formulated plan, was a piecemeal advance to relieve the various fortresses of the Bar-Lev Line. During the evening and night of 6/7 October, Israeli tank brigades made several desperate ventures, often on the basis of incomplete information. Typically such sallies ended when the tanks found themselves in the midst of Egyptian infantry and showered by *Sagger* missiles. Losses were very heavy. Shomron's tank brigade, for example, which fought on a 35-mile front after emerging from the Gidi and Mitla passes, lost about 75 of its 100-odd tanks during that night.

Due not so much to bad communications but rather to careless and negligent reporting, the Israeli command at this stage had an incomplete and mainly optimistic impression of the situation. It was only on the Sunday morning, when it was reported that about two-thirds of the tanks had been lost and no ground regained, that the gravity of the events became apparent. Dayan then appears to have become depressed with the whole situation, openly forecasting a great Israeli retreat. However, his subordinates in the field did not follow his recommendations for withdrawal. On the Tuesday, Golda Meir intervened to prevent him giving a television account of the previous days' fighting, sending a more reticent and optimistic general instead.

On 7 October, with the first reservists swelling the available forces, three divisional headquarters were set up to handle the situation on this front. 'Bren' Adan looked after the northern sector, the central sector was entrusted to a division commanded by Arik Sharon, while in the south, from Great Bitter Lake to Suez, the line was completed by Avraham Mandler's division, which hitherto had been responsible for the whole length, and was recovering from the previous night's disasters. In overall command of this, the Southern Front, was Shmuel Gonen. A massive Israeli counterattack launched on 7 October was a costly failure. It consisted of a southern sweep by Adan's division but this was carried out too far to the east, so instead of folding up the Egyptian line in a flanking attack it merely passed along the front of the Egyptian positions, where its armored brigades fell victim to antitank guns and missiles. Because Adan's division seemed to be moving quite fast, Gonen thought the attack was going well, so he ordered Sharon's division to move in preparation for joining in. But when Gonen realized that the attack was failing, he ordered Sharon to go back from where he had started, with the result that on this crucial day Sharon's men moved backward and forward without doing any fighting. This no doubt irritated Sharon, and there began a period of bickering between Israeli generals that would have been unseemly at the best of times, but was remarkable at a time of crisis.

Sharon had been Gonen's predecessor as the officer commanding the Southern Front, and had retired shortly before this war. He immediately returned to service, and was appointed a divisional commander. He had a reputation as a brave and wily officer, but had poor relationships with his colleagues, some of whom distrusted him while others regarded him as an opportunist. His friends said that his fault was that he did not like taking orders, especially when he believed his own proposals were better (they often were) or when his superior was a man whom he did not like. His reputation as a deceiver probably derived from the subterfuges he sometimes employed to disguise his defiance of instructions. The day after Sharon had been irritated by Gonen's apparent misuse of his division, he made an attack on an Egyptian position despite Gonen's order not to do so: Gonen then asked the Chief of Staff to dismiss Sharon. The Chief of Staff, Elazar, did not comply. Instead he sent the retired Chaim Bar-Lev, now a government minister, to take command of the Southern Front, with Gonen as his subordinate. Bar-Lev soon proposed that Sharon be dismissed, but Dayan twice refused this request, so Sharon stayed on, and had a glorious war.

Meanwhile, the war continued, and was going badly for the Israelis. Because of the Syrian attack in the north, the full Israeli potential could not be brought to bear against the Egyptians, and the war-winning techniques of previous campaigns were no longer effective. Not only could Egyptian infantry cope with Israeli tanks, but the Israelis were deprived of the air support which they badly needed. In the early days of the war the Egyptian Air Force, for the most part, stayed in the concrete hangars that had been built to prevent a repetition of the 1967 debacle. It flew ground-support missions, but not in large numbers because the Army was so well-equipped with guns and missiles that it had little need of aircraft. At the same time, the Army's air-defense system of SAM-2, SAM-3 and SAM-6 missiles, supported by the Soviet-built ZSU-23-4 multifrequency radar-controlled rapid-fire antiaircraft gun, was proving a match for the Israeli ground-attack aircraft. On the first day the Israelis suffered serious losses in Phantom and Skyhawk machines. The SAM system was advanced as the Egyptians moved forward: screens of SAM-6

LEFT: *Israeli Centurion tanks throw up clouds of sand as they advance in the Sinai.*

ABOVE: *A Syrian Air Force MiG-17 overflies advancing Syrian troops.*
RIGHT: *Syria's advance in the Golan.*

attacks across the Canal. Meanwhile, the Syrians were also making good progress; their plan had been less complex, envisaging an advance by infantry with strong tank support, with the main armor held back until the chance of a major breakthrough presented itself.

As the Syrians were much closer to Israel proper than the Egyptians, the Israelis devoted most of their air strength to the Northern Front – in particular to intensive strikes in the Golan Heights, where the Syrian attack was concentrated. The Syrians did possess some SAM missiles, but to a lesser extent than did Egypt, so the Israeli aircraft, though suffering losses, were able to inflict serious damage on the Syrian army. This, however was not enough to stop the Syrian advance. On the second day the Syrians launched their armored divisions in the hope of making deep penetrations.

missiles were placed ahead, with SAM-2 or SAM-3 launchers behind them. This pattern was not impenetrable, but the Israelis soon came to realize that the percentage of aircraft losses meant that only the most vital or urgent targets were worth attacking. An additional hazard were the bazooka-type antiaircraft missiles (SAM-7) used by the Egyptian infantry; these were not very accurate, and their charges were often not lethal, but they were enough to distract pilots at times when attention to targeting was important. During the war, on both fronts, about 120 Israeli aircraft were shot down, and about 80 of these were the victims of SAM-6 missiles. As previously, in aerial combat the Israelis were superior, and lost few planes to Egyptian pilots.

In the main, the Egyptian intentions for the first days of the campaign were fulfilled, and at a much smaller loss than expected. In particular, the hazardous crossing of the Canal, in which many Egyptian commanders expected to sustain casualties to at least a third of their men, was accomplished with small loss. By Tuesday the Egyptians had two bridgeheads on the eastern bank, six or seven miles deep, and apparently secure from Israeli armor and air attack. Numerous bridges had been built across the Canal and Israeli air attacks, which to some extent were concentrated against these bridges, had resulted in serious aircraft losses. The ease with which the Russian-made bridges could be repaired and shifted meant that no lasting damage was caused. As planned, some medium tanks had crossed the Canal, although for the time being reserves of armor were retained on the western bank to thwart any possible Israeli counter-

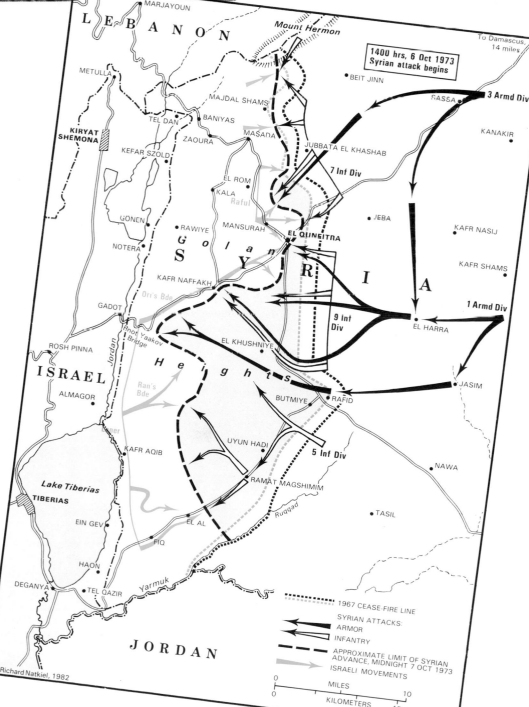

ABOVE: *An Israeli 175mm self-propelled howitzer shells Syrian positions on the Golan Heights, 11 October 1973.*
LEFT: *An Israeli Centurion tank moves up to reinforce positions on the Golan Heights.*

Moral justification, of sorts, for the Israeli decision to bomb civilian targets was provided by the Syrian use of *Frog* rockets in the first days of the war. Presumably aimed at the Ramat David airfield, these small unguided missiles had mostly landed elsewhere, in some cases damaging Israeli settlements.

Considerable damage was inflicted on oil installations; the Israeli Navy co-operated on the Mediterranean coast by bombarding Latakia and Tartous. Power stations at Damascus and Homs were put out of action. Attacks on central Damascus were less successful; bombs intended for the defense ministry buildings in the center of the capital hit the Soviet cultural center instead, killing a Russian civilian. The resulting diplomatic embarrassment persuaded Dayan that attacks on Damascus were not such a good idea after all. The Israeli Navy had a similar unfortunate experience when bombarding Tartous; Israeli missiles aimed at Syrian warships hit a Soviet freighter instead, and sank it. Syria appealed to Egypt, and then Iraq, to launch retributive air attacks on Israeli civilian targets, but both governments, while sympathetic, decided to take no action.

Meanwhile, the Israeli Army had found the weak point it had been seeking in the Golan Heights, and in a rapid advance reached Sassa, halfway to Damascus, by 13 October. At this point, however, the Syrians rallied, helped in large part by

But on 9 October the tide unexpectedly turned in the Golan Heights. The immediate cause of the halt of the Syrian advance and its eventual reversal was an ammunition shortage which crippled the Syrian SAM-6 missile sites. As the Syrians began to conserve their missiles, Israeli aircraft had better opportunities of attacking the sites themselves, and the only immediate solution was for the Syrians to evacuate a proportion of their launchers. This situation encouraged the Israeli command to make an all-out effort against Syria, with the aim of knocking it out of the war so as to permit a final concentration of forces against the Egyptians. In a

new departure, Syria was subjected to strategic bombing directed against communications, electricity supply, and industry. Syrian SAM sites were mainly on the Plain of Damascus, leaving several avenues of approach open to the Israeli aircraft. Moreover, Syrian industry and electric power stations were located close together within Syria, simplifying targeting. At the same time as this attack on the Syrian economy and Syrian civilian morale was launched, the Israeli army in the Golan Heights shifted from a broad-front to a narrow-front strategy, with the aim of a breakthrough of concentrated forces toward Damascus.

their allies. They reorganized themselves on a new defensive line based on Sassa, and benefited from the arrival of troops sent from Jordan, Iraq, Morocco and Kuwait. The 40th Jordanian Tank Brigade was an exceptionally valuable acquisition, as it was well trained and familiar with the terrain. Although in the subsequent battles, the Jordanians and, especially, the Iraqis, suffered substantial losses of tanks, the damage inflicted on the Israelis was sufficient to persuade them that further advance would be too costly. The Syrians, who even as early as 9 October had lost about 600 of their tanks, were considerably helped by the Russians. After some hesitation, Moscow had decided to re-supply both Syria and Egypt while the war was still progressing; without this, both the Syrians and Egyptians would have been obliged to cease fire within a week of

RIGHT: *Israeli Chief of Staff, General Elazar (third left), on the Syrian front.*
BELOW: *A Syrian infantryman brings his RPG-7 antitank rocket launcher into action near Mount Hermon.*

the start of the war. Soviet stocks from Eastern Europe, airlifted via Hungary, seem to have been the first to arrive, and sea deliveries from Odessa followed soon after. At about the same time the US government began to organize an air- and

BELOW: *A map illustrating the Israeli counterattack over the Suez Canal.*
BELOW RIGHT: *Destroyed Egyptian T-55 (left) tank lies derelict beside a knocked-out Israeli upgraded M48 in the Sinai.*
INSET: *The Egyptian General Saad el Shazli.*

sea-lift to resupply Israel. To save Syrian tank crews for combat, Soviet personnel drove newly delivered tanks from the ports to the battlefield and, unlike in Egypt, Soviet military advisers accompanied Syrian units in the frontline. Thanks to Soviet ammunition resupply, Israeli troops in Syria were subjected to unprecedented volumes of artillery fire in terms of shells per mile of front. (In absolute terms, Egypt's opening bombardment on 6 October probably remained the record, when in the first minute the Israeli defenses were struck by 175 shells

per second.) A Red Navy destroyer patrolled off Latakia to deter Israeli submarine attacks on supply ships, and some of the missile sites protecting Damascus were manned by Russians.

In view of the stiffening Syrian resistance, the Israeli command decided to accept a stalemate on this front, enabling at least some of the effort to be transferred to Sinai. Here the Egyptians, perhaps taken aback by the totality of their success, had lost impetus, and were about to renew it with an offensive which was an unhappy compromise between boldness and

caution. Possibly the need to do something to help Syria affected the judgment of the Egyptian command. Certainly Soviet envoys in Cairo were painting a grim picture, even suggesting that Damascus was about to drop out of the war.

On 13 October, therefore, the Egyptian armored divisions, hitherto held in reserve on the western bank of the Canal, were brought forward in preparation for an attack on the Mitla and Gidi passes. It seems that President Sadat had been urging this operation, supported by the War Minister, while Chief of Staff Shazli

had resisted it. The Second and Third Egyptian Armies holding the eastern bank thereby received an accretion of strength, the 21st Armored Division going to the former and the 4th Armored Division to the latter. Only one armored brigade was left on the western bank. About 1000 tanks had been sent to the eastern bank already, in support of the infantry, and the new arrivals probably totalled about 600 units. With the tank losses suffered by both sides, numbers of tanks in service in the armored units was well below establishment, so 600 tanks

was a weighty contribution.

The Egyptian attack began at dawn on 14 October. Three armored thrusts were made by the Third Army and three by the Second. The ultimate object of the Egyptian plan was a broad pincer movement directed toward Bir Gafgafa, and a capture of the passes was part of this. In the north the 18th Infantry Division, with a tank brigade, advanced from Kantara toward Rumani. In the center, opposing Sharon's division, the 21st Armored Division, with some help from a tank brigade of the 23rd Mechanized

Division, advanced from the Egyptian bridgehead opposite Ismailia. Further south, in the area covered by the division commanded by Kalman Magen (since Mandler's death in a missile attack) one Egyptian tank brigade moved toward the Gidi Pass and a second toward the Mitla Pass. Further south, a mixed task force was to push south along the Gulf of Suez in an attempt to capture Ras Sudar.

As the distances separating these thrusts were quite small, the offensive soon resolved itself into a series of tank engagements constituting the largest tank battle since the Battle of Kursk in 1943. As soon became apparent, the Egyptians were at a great disadvantage. Firstly, because they advanced outside the cover of their SAM missile systems and were therefore at the mercy of the Israeli Air Force; little

effective protection could be offered by the Egyptian Air Force. Secondly, as this was a fast-moving battle, the infantry with its deadly *Sagger* antitank missiles was soon left behind, removing the most serious threat to the Israeli tanks. When the opposing tank forces engaged, Israeli formations came out best. A particularly big engagement took place around the Mitla Pass where Magen's tanks, aided by paratroopers, almost completely destroyed one armored brigade, while the Israeli Air Force wreaked havoc on others. When the day's count was completed it appeared that on this front the Egyptians had lost about 250 tanks against a mere 10 on the Israeli side; General Mamoun, commander of the Egyptian Second Army, had a heart attack. In Cairo the extent of the disaster was concealed throughout the

day by the scarcity and false optimism of the messages being sent back from the two armies, and it was only in the evening that the futility of dispatching tanks without missile protection was realized. By then it was too late, and the surviving Egyptian tanks were hurrying back to the positions from which they had begun the day's activities. Later, the Egyptians ascribed the defeat largely to French-supplied Israeli antitank guided missiles.

The transfer of the Egyptian armor reserves from the Western to the eastern bank of the Canal was a signal for the Israeli command to prepare a counterstroke that had been under discussion for some days. This was to be a crossing in force to the western bank, thereby taking the Egyptian forces from the rear and changing the whole course of the war in

BELOW: *Israeli Centurion tanks advance to attack Syrian positions on the Golan Heights.*

Israel's favor. Despite the urging of certain generals, including Sharon, to begin such a move at once, as soon as enough forces had been accumulated, it was decided to wait until the Egyptian armor had been shifted eastward, as such a move seemed imminent. On 9 October, more or less by accident, an Israeli reconnaissance force had discovered that the boundary between the Egyptian Second and Third armies lay across the Great Bitter Lake, and that the western side of the Lake was undefended. It was therefore decided that the Israeli crossing would be best attempted at that location. A first objective, once across, would be a rapid movement along the western bank to destroy SAM missile sites, thereby creating avenues of approach for the Israeli ground-attack aircraft.

Sharon's division was entrusted with the operation, which began in the late afternoon of 15 October. Assault boats carried paratroopers across, and they had little difficulty in establishing a bridgehead. Both Egyptian armies on the eastern bank reacted by closing the gap between them but were held apart by the Israelis at the Battle of Chinese Farm. This Egyptian response, together with mix-ups over the movement of bridging gear, delayed the building of the first bridge but on 16 October a few tanks and armored personnel carriers were taken over to begin the attacks on the missile sites. Adan's division joined Sharon's and eventually a pontoon bridge was placed across the water. Adan's arrival proved timely, for it destroyed the Egyptian 25th Armored Brigade, which attacked on the eastern

shore from the south. On the western bank resistance was slight, because there were few Egyptian forces available. Also, the seriousness of the situation was not conveyed to the Egyptian command, which continued to regard this ever-increasing influx of Israeli troops as just a raid. Soon the remaining Israeli division, Magen's, also joined in so that the bulk of the Israeli Southern Front forces was located on the western bank, while the bulk of the Egyptian forces remained on the eastern bank, only hazily aware of what was happening. To block any possible Egyptian advance eastward, which was considered unlikely, the Israeli command had left a newly formed division of reservists, with one of Sharon's brigades to defend the Chinese Farm area, and a mixed force from Magen's division to watch the Third Army.

It was only on 17 October that the Israeli bridgehead came under serious fire, from guns, missiles and aircraft. The air attacks were usually beaten off by Israeli fighters, which were relatively untroubled by SAM missiles, since the sites had been cleared by the land forces. Egyptian commandos also made desperate attacks, and at times fighting was heavy, but the bridgehead was never really threatened with abandonment. According to Shazli, the Egyptian Chief of Staff had earlier recommended a return to the western bank of the armor reserves, and was not in favor of the general deployment of forces imposed by Sadat. Shazli, it seems, was among the first to realize that the situation was potentially catastrophic, but had great difficulty in persuading Sadat, who at one point threatened him with a court-martial if he insisted on arguing (after the war Shazli denounced Sadat and took up residence in Libya). It was only when Soviet Prime Minister Kosygin arrived in Cairo and showed Sadat satellite pictures of the Israeli formations on the western bank that Sadat began to realize the enormity of the situation which now faced him. By this time Moscow was in favor of a ceasefire, rightly considering that Egypt and Syria had attained the objective of improving their negotiating position and proving that they were a formidable military combination as far as Israel was concerned. It seemed to the Soviet general staff as they surveyed the situation, that any extension of hostilities could only result in a deterioration of the Syrian-Egyptian position.

On 18 October the Israelis had finally prevailed in the Chinese Farm area, in some of the heaviest and most persistent fighting of the whole campaign. Their eastern base area being safe, they had built more bridges and were assured of supplies. Throughout 19 October their forces on the western bank concentrated on a drive toward Suez, while the Egyptian Third Army, on the opposite bank, was held down by air attacks. A paratroop drop the following day captured Fayid Airport. On 21 October the Cairo–Suez road was reached, thereby cutting a main communication artery, and Sharon's men had driven north almost as far as Ismailia. These advances threatened to cut off the Egyptian armies on the eastern bank. The Egyptian Third Army, in particular, was close to encirclement, and it was in order to complete this encirclement (thereby

© Richard Natkiel, 1982

gaining an important bargaining counter in the negotiations which clearly would begin in the following few days) that the Israelis on 23 October broke the ceasefire that had been arranged by the USA and USSR. This permitted the capture of Ras Adabiah, and although Egyptian resistance in Suez prevented the capture of that town, the Israeli advance had been substantial enough to completely isolate the Egyptian Third Army. It was at this point that the fighting ceased. In the meantime, on the Syrian front, fighting had been fierce but inconclusive. If anything, despite Syrian counterattacks, the Israelis had made small gains, with Mount Hermon being taken on 22 October.

The war at sea was pursued more actively than in previous campaigns. Moreover, although the ships were small and the engagements short, the war witnessed

FAR LEFT: *The map shows Israeli counterattacks into Syria.*
BELOW: *A Syrian Army T-55 tank, fitted with mine-clearing rollers, rests by a roadside.*

the first large-scale use of the guided missile in naval warfare. The main Israeli strength consisted of 14 missile boats, although there were submarines as well. They faced an Egyptian Navy of two submarines, five destroyers, and more significantly, eight *Osa* and six *Komar* boats armed with *Styx* missiles, and about 30 motor torpedo boats. In addition, the Syrians had six *Komar* boats.

The Battle of Latakia occurred on the night of 6/7 October, when five Israeli missile boats encountered the Syrians off that port. The Israelis first met a torpedo boat, which they sank, then a minesweeper, also quickly disposed of, and then three missile craft. A half-hour battle, involving an exchange of missiles, ended when all three of the Syrian boats went to the bottom. This victory enabled the Israel Navy to dominate the Syrian coast, at least at night, leading to Syrian fears of an amphibious landing, and thereby tying down the armored brigade which they allocated to defend this coast.

On the following night a force of six Israeli missile boats that approached the Egyptian Mediterranean coastline at Damiette, west of Port Said, in order to bombard military targets, was intercepted by four opposing missile boats. Although outranged, the Israelis persisted and eventually their missiles sank three of the Egyptian craft. Presumably the Israeli success in these battles was assisted by

superior electronic countermeasures, but few details were made public. In the Gulf of Suez, where the Egyptians could in theory dispatch two destroyers that they had based on Aden, and a couple of submarines based on Port Sudan, the small Israeli craft were able to disrupt ferry traffic which had been intended to provide a service across the Gulf for the benefit of the Egyptian armies. There were a couple of engagements in which Egyptian small craft were sunk, but in general the result of this naval campaign was that both sides were able to deny use of the Gulf of Suez to the other.

The refusal of the Israelis to observe the original ceasefire caused considerable alarm in Moscow, which feared that a total defeat of Egypt, and hence a serious setback for the USSR, was about to ensue. This caused a somewhat more brusque tone to be adopted in communications with Washington, and the US government, either because it was badly advised or refused to listen to advice, responded with an Alert signal to its armed forces. This alert was called a 'nuclear alert' by the Western press, a misleading though not inaccurate description. In general it was viewed as an over-reaction casting further doubt on Washington's ability to respond rationally to Soviet behavior. For Western governments, this was one unnerving event of the Yom Kippur War. Another was the use by the Arab states of the long-

discussed 'oil weapon' to put pressure on the West. When the decision to use an oil embargo, with its concomitant price-rise, was taken, the results of the move had been insufficiently studied. The result was that, although it was intended as a means of putting pressure on the USA to restrain Israel, its main beneficiaries were the American oil companies, which had long wanted to raise prices and which in addition were granted a useful argument in their battle with the environmentalist movement. The worst-hit were Japan and the countries of Western Europe which, with the possible exception of the Netherlands, had not been regarded as hostile by the Arabs.

In the Yom Kippur War, Israel could claim to be the military victor, but Egypt, Syria and the Arab cause in general were clearly the political victors. They had won a position of strength which, before long, would persuade the Israelis to leave Sinai. The USA, too, had improved its position. US assistance with the ceasefire arrangements and with the rescue of the Egyptian Third Army from its perilous, water-short, situation, brought Sadat into closer touch with America and before long he turned Egypt back toward a Western orientation.

BELOW: *Captured Syrian Army T-62 tanks.* RIGHT: *A Finnish soldier of the UN watches a truck set on fire by withdrawing Israeli troops, 1974.*

CRISIS IN
THE LEBANON

The initial Egyptian successes in the Yom Kippur War had as deep an impact on Israeli public opinion as they did in the Arab world. The government set up an official commission of enquiry, the Agranat Commission, whose findings led to a number of changes. Some of these were personal; although Dayan was not criticized, Chief of Staff Elazar was, and had to quit office. The Director, and three other high Military Intelligence officers, were also removed. Military Intelligence was subsequently enlarged in the hope that it would do better in future. The peacetime strength of the IDF was enhanced by a large increase in the number of units maintained at full strength. Reserve forces were strengthened by calling up a higher proportion of those eligible. There was continuing investment in more modern weapons, with the beginning of domestic production of more sophisticated items. Among them were the Merkova tank and the Kfir aircraft (home-built, on the basis of the Mirage airframe and an American engine).

Within a few years of the Yom Kippur War, therefore, Israel possessed an even stronger IDF. However, professionalization to a large extent meant an end to the spontaneity and enterprise of the old days, when units were small and improvisation and local decision making were key elements. Israel was beginning to be a military power, possessor of a war machine, but was not quite sure what to do with this strength. Meanwhile, the nature of the state of Israel had changed, largely under the pressure of three decades of war. Israel no longer resembled the state which the pioneers had intended to establish as a national home. Partly because of the wars, partly because of the influx of Jews expelled from Arab countries whose attitudes and aspirations were far different from those of the European Jews, the spirit of the country had changed. It had become uncompromising, ungenerous, and too eager to view situations in military rather than human terms. For many Israelis of the old type, the emergence of an unrepentant former terrorist, Menachem Begin, as Prime Minister, was a symbol of this deterioration. Yet it was Begin who, because of his reputation as a hard and uncompromising character, was able to persuade the Israelis to make a peace with Egypt that involved Israel's evacuation of the Sinai Peninsula.

After the 1973 ceasefire, Israel was obliged to pull back its forces rather farther than it would have liked. US support at this time was weak, partly because the Arab states' oil weapon seemed quite threatening, and partly because Washington was already feeling its way toward an accommodation with Sadat that might pull Egypt out of the Soviet sphere of influence. Whereas Israel was able to retain the vital Golan Heights, in Sinai

there was a withdrawal to a line east of the Gidi and Mitla passes and extending almost to El Tur; the oilfields near El Tur, however, remained in Israeli hands. This was only a ceasefire line, and international (mainly US) pressure was directed toward a more permanent settlement. The unquelled and indeed intensifying *Fedayeen* activity, together with the heavy economic burden of maintaining readiness for a possible Egyptian assault, also induced the Israelis to seek a long-term settlement.

In November 1977, after some com-

PREVIOUS PAGES: *Beirut under attack by Israeli artillery and aircraft, August 1982.*
TOP: *A youth dashes for cover during a firefight between Christian militiamen and PLO and Muslim forces in Beirut, 1975.*
RIGHT: *Egyptian General Gamasy arrives at Km 101 in Sinai for disengagement talks in 1974.*
BELOW: *General Elazar arrives at Km 101 to sign the disengagement agreement, 1974.*

promising words by Begin in a radio broadcast, Sadat surprised the world, and not least his own people, by flying to Israel and speaking to the *Knesset* (parliament). However, despite this emotional breakthrough, it soon became evident that Begin would not be a magnanimous negotiator. Sadat wished to negotiate a settlement that would be acceptable to his former allies Syria and Jordan. Begin was intent on making peace with Egypt and, having thereby secured his rear, continuing to consolidate the Israeli position in the Syrian and Jordanian areas occupied by Israeli troops. His object was to incorporate into Israel territory won by force of arms, and his method was the time-honored strategy of settlement. In the West Bank, which Begin soon claimed was

ABOVE RIGHT: *Henry Kissinger (right) talks to Abba Eban (left) and Yigal Allon during his 'shuttle diplomacy' which led to a settlement between Israel and Egypt in 1979.*
RIGHT: *Jimmy Carter stands between Menachem Begin and Anwar Sadat during the Camp David conference.*
BELOW: *Part of the Ghanaian contingent of the UN peacekeeping force on the Suez Canal.*

by historical necessity an integral part of the Jewish inheritance, a campaign of Jewish immigration was started. Among other things, this entailed the building of Jewish settlements on Arab land at a time when the policy of the Israeli army of occupation was to win the hearts and minds of the local Arabs by fair and generous treatment. Jewish settlement of the West Bank, therefore, not only aroused the fury of Arabs and the criticism of Western countries, but also disturbed a large number of Israelis. However, Begin had the votes, which is what counts in a democracy.

In fact, an Israel-Egypt Peace Treaty was finally worked out, signed and implemented. The Camp David Agreement of 1979, reached under the auspices of President Carter, was the prelude to this. The Treaty was the first treaty, as opposed to armistice, signed by Israel with its Arab neighbors, and as such it attracted much hostility in the Arab world. At Camp David, Begin's Molotov-style stonewalling had aroused long-lasting American criticism, but it resulted in an agreement which satisfied Israel's main object without giving away more than was strictly necessary. That is largely why Sadat's wish to include Syria and Jordan in the settlement was disappointed. All the same, Israel's concession of a return of all Sinai to Egypt was not insubstantial, for not only did this remove a wide buffer zone, it also sacrificed the increasingly valuable oilfields of El Tur. The Israeli withdrawal was in three phases, and it was not until the last was completed in 1982 that Cairo could be certain that the Israeli side of the Treaty would be kept. Jewish settlements had been built in Sinai as well as on the West Bank, though on a smaller scale. Both the sponsors of these settlements, who included expansionist-minded politicians of some weight, and the inhabitants, resisted their dissolution. It was only the evident willingness of the government to use the

LEFT: *The Camp David accords led to a close friendship between Egypt and the US.*
BELOW LEFT: *Soviet supplied Mi-8 assault helicopters remained in Egyptian service after the withdrawal of Soviet aid.*
RIGHT: *Israeli M113 armored personnel carriers on the road to Tyre during the invasion of Southern Lebanon in 1982.*
BELOW RIGHT: *Israeli mobile units approach Beirut.*

Army against resisters that persuaded the settlers to give up and return to Israel-proper. Begin's judgment was sound on this issue; if a long-term peace with Egypt was obtainable by sacrificing a tract of desert, it was well worth it. The loss of some oil production was substantial, but its economic effect was far smaller than the economic gain obtained by eliminating the need to remain ready, year after year, for war with Egypt. For Egypt there were similar economic advantages, but Sadat paid the price of extreme unpopularity in Arab capitals and virtual ostracization. His assassination in 1981, which took place when he was celebrating the anniversary of the Yom Kippur War, was the work not of hostile Arab governments but of domestic fundamentalists.

In the negotiating processes Sadat came into close contact with Washington, and it was not long before he turned to the West for military help. In any case it would have been difficult to maintain good relations with the USSR after the peace with Israel. This peace left Syria resentful and dependent on the Soviet Union, the relationship becoming closer as Egypt-Soviet relations worsened. The Egyptian change of direction meant that the armed forces once again had to make the expensive and difficult transition from one arms supplier to another. Maintenance of existing Soviet-built equipment was a major problem, but by the late 1970s British technicians were servicing Soviet-built jet engines and Soviet-built tanks. Britain also became a considerable arms supplier, particularly in the field of anti-tank and antiaircraft missiles. Non-Soviet jet aircraft joined the Egyptian Air Force, beginning with a batch of F-5 interceptors from the USA and Mirages from France.

The peace with Egypt not only relieved Israel of a heavy military commitment, but also eliminated a large part of the *Fedayeen* problem, armed incursions henceforth coming only from Syria, Jordan and Lebanon. However, from the late 1960s the activities of the PLO had increasingly taken an international direction. Israeli targets were attacked overseas where they were less well-protected and where any terrorist successes would be well-publicized. The hijacking of aircraft became prevalent, and for a time highly successful. An El Al airliner hijacked to Algeria in 1968 marked the beginning of this phase, and soon Israeli diplomats,

officials and establishments abroad came under attack. The murder of several members of the Israeli team at the 1972 Munich Olympic Games gained the expected volume of publicity. The same year there was a terrorist attack at Lod Airport, inside Israel. This is notable because it was carried out by a Japanese 'Red Army' group. It succeeded only in killing many travellers, mainly Puerto Ricans, and emphasized the links which were developing between the Palestinian PLO and terrorist organizations in other countries.

The Israeli response to all kinds of attack was unbending. In the case of *Fedayeen* raids, retribution on a larger scale than the original attack was inevitable. With hijacking, the policy was to refuse all demands made by the terrorists in return for the release of hostages and, wherever possible, to attack the terrorists so that future attackers would know that they faced almost certain death. In some cases this resulted in more deaths of

innocents than would otherwise have occurred, but it achieved its aim of making armed blackmail an unproductive method insofar as Israeli citizens were concerned. This policy was also applied to hostage-taking raids inside Israel itself. When in 1974 terrorists held children hostage in an Israeli school in Galilee the Israeli Army immediately attacked, killing more

LEFT: *An Israeli patrol drives through the Shia Muslim village of Zabkin in southern Lebanon, during their operations to clear the Palestinian guerrillas south of the Litani River in 1978.*
BELOW: *A French-designed AML-90 Panhard armored car of the UN Forces in Lebanon supervises the Israeli withdrawal, June 1978.*

children than terrorists but achieving the larger object of deterrence. The high point of Israeli counterterrorist policy came with the freeing of the passengers of an Air France plane carrying Jewish passengers that had been hijacked to Entebbe. There were precedents for this, including the 1972 recapture of a Belgian airliner taken over by terrorists and immobilized at Ben-Gurion Airport in Israel.

The Entebbe operation was a triumph for the IDF's special unit that had been trained for this kind of work. This unit, together with a refined intelligence service, was Israel's main weapon against major terrorist operations. The airliner had been hijacked to Entebbe by a mixed Palestin-

ian and German group of terrorists, and the passengers were interned under guard in an airport building. As at this time relations between President Amin of Uganda and Israel were bad, there seemed little hope of extracting the hostages by diplomacy, and to accept the terrorists' demand (for the release of about 50 terrorists imprisoned in various countries) was, as usual, considered out of the question. Sending Israeli transport aircraft to Entebbe, landing special-unit troops there, and then taking off after rescuing the hostages, was formidably difficult. But good intelligence, intricate planning, sheer

LEFT: *An Egyptian Army BTR-50 amphibious personnel carrier pictured in 1980.*
INSET FAR LEFT: *An Israeli M109 self-propelled 155mm howitzer takes up position between apartment blocks in Beirut, 1982.*
BELOW: *A map showing Israeli operations in southern Lebanon.*

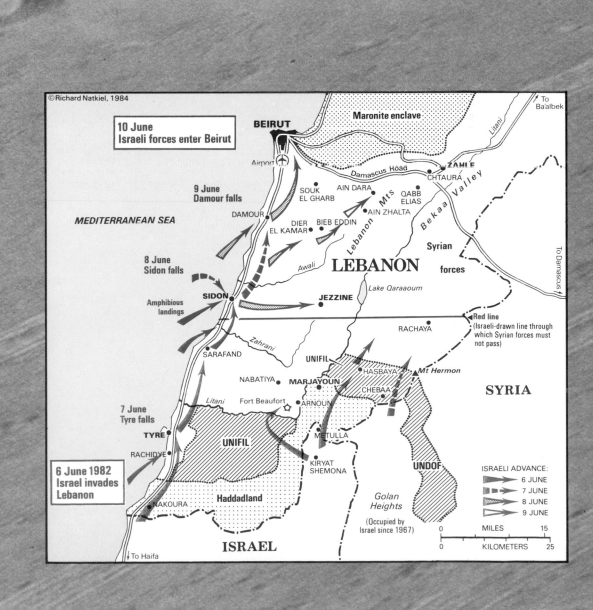

© Richard Natkiel, 1984

10 June
Israeli forces enter Beirut

BEIRUT

Maronite enclave

To Ba'albek

Airport

Damascus Road

ZAHLE

CHTAURA

9 June
Damour falls

SOUK EL GHARB

AIN DARA

QABB ELIAS

MEDITERRANEAN SEA

DAMOUR

DIER EL KAMAR

BIEB EDDIN

AIN ZHALTA

Bekaa Valley

To Damascus

LEBANON

Awali

Syrian forces

8 June
Sidon falls

Lake Qaraaoum

Amphibious landings

SIDON

JEZZINE

Red line
(Israeli-drawn line through which Syrian forces must not pass)

RACHAYA

Zahrani

SARAFAND

UNIFIL

SYRIA

NABATIYA

MARJAYOUN

HASBAYA

▲ Mt Hermon

CHEBAA

7 June
Tyre falls

Litani

Fort Beaufort

ARNOUN

METULLA

UNDOF

TYRE

RACHIDYE

UNIFIL

KIRYAT SHEMONA

6 June 1982
Israel invades Lebanon

NAKOURA

Haddadland

Golan Heights
(Occupied by Israel since 1967)

ISRAELI ADVANCE:

6 JUNE
7 JUNE
8 JUNE
9 JUNE

0   MILES   15
0   KILOMETERS   25

ISRAEL

To Haifa

competence on the ground, and an absence of bad luck, all combined to make the operation a complete success. The terrorists were killed either while guarding the hostages or while sleeping, only a few Ugandan troops were killed, and the hostages were brought back to Israel.

How far terrorist activity based in Lebanon was a reason or a pretext for the Israeli invasion of that country is uncertain. It is fairly clear that, after making peace with Egypt, Begin intended to tackle what he regarded as the next essential objectives. First was the elimination of terrorist attacks and second, linked to this, was the creation of firm frontiers which would enclose what Begin considered to be the proper territory of a future, secure, Israel. This territory would include the West Bank, to be made Jewish, and territory in the Lebanese and Syrian frontier areas which would make those frontiers more secure.

LEFT: *The Kfir C-2 fighter was developed by Israel Aircraft Industries from the Mirage III.*
RIGHT: *Israeli infantry in the Lebanon.*
BELOW RIGHT: *An Israeli reconnaissance drone shot down over Lebanon.*
BELOW: *Israeli troops became involved in street fighting in Beirut in August 1982.*

In 1978 the PLO, based in Lebanon, made a seaborne raid on Israel and hijacked a bus. In the ensuing action with the IDF, most of the passengers were hurt, 36 fatally. Retribution for this was on an unprecedented scale, and amounted to an invasion of southern Lebanon by about 25,000 Israeli troops. Hundreds of people, described by the Israelis as PLO members, were killed by tanks, guns and aircraft. A certain quantity of terrorist equipment was captured, some of it comprising large items like antitank guns, but the number of genuine terrorists killed or captured was small. At that time Lebanon, largely because of the strain caused by the presence of thousands of PLO supporters, was disintegrating as a state, and Syrian troops were present in a fairly genuine peacekeeping role. The Syrians, among other things, deterred a long Israel advance northward, so the Litani River was regarded by both Israelis and Syrians as a boundary separating Israeli-occupied Lebanon from the rest of that country. Eventually a UN force was sent to occupy the Litani area so as to encourage the Israelis to withdraw.

Israel gave what support it could to two of the Lebanese factions, the Phalangists (militant right-wing Christians) and the Christians under the banner of Major Saad Haddad. Haddad maintained an enclave of his own in southern Lebanon, just north of the Israeli frontier, so his goodwill was important. Despite the presence of the UN troops (UNIFIL),

Israeli forces remained active in Lebanon, fighting mainly the PLO but sometimes the Syrians. In April 1981 Israeli aircraft shot down two Syrian helicopters in the Bekaa Valley of Lebanon while operating in support of the Phalangists. Perhaps in response to this, Syria deployed SAM-6 missiles in the Bekaa Valley, and for a time these kept the Israelis away. Meanwhile, in an effort to dislodge the PLO from Lebanon, Israeli aircraft that summer attacked positions believed to be held by the PLO. Hundreds of civilians were killed by Israeli attacks on West Beirut, and in due course the PLO replied with a rocket attack on targets inside Israeli territory.

This outburst of fighting was halted, for nine months, by a UN ceasefire in late

LEFT: *Troops move into wrecked buildings during the street fighting in Beirut.*
BELOW: *A TV cameraman in Beirut.*

July, Israel agreeing to refrain from air attacks against Lebanese territory. On 3 June an assassination attempt was made on the Israeli Ambassador in London, Shlomo Argov. This was the catalyst for a massive Israeli operation which amounted to a full-scale war; with Begin as Prime Minister and Arik Sharon as Defense Minister, the Israeli government intended to exploit its military power. The operation which brought renewed war, called 'Operation Peace for Galilee,' involved a three-pronged northward advance by Israeli forces, which totalled about 90,000 men. The main attack was along the coastal road, reaching the outskirts of Beirut while mastering Tyre and Damour, and moving to cut the Beirut-Damascus highway. The second prong captured from the

LEFT: *The Israeli withdrawal in Lebanon.*
TOP RIGHT: *Begin visits Washington.*
RIGHT: *Israeli shells explode along the seafront at Beirut.*

Map

BEIRUT

WEST (Muslim) EAST (Christian)

HQ. French paratroops

SABRA AND CHATILA REFUGEE CAMPS

Italian troops

Damascus Road

HQ. British troops

HQ. US marines

Airport

0 MILES 2
0 KM 3

16 Sept 1982
Christian militia massacre of Palestinians in Sabra and Chatila refugee camps

18 April 1983
US embassy bombed
23 Oct
US and French headquarters blown up

To Ba'albek

Maronite enclave

BEIRUT

21 Aug-1 Sept 1982
Syrian and PLO forces evacuate Beirut

ALEY   Damascus   ZAHLE
SOUK EL GHARB   AIN DARA
Chouf
DAMOUR   BHAMDOUN   Barouk Peak

Bekaa Valley   Road

4 Sept 1983
Israeli forces withdraw to Awali river

Awali

SIDON   Lake Qaraaoum

JEZZINE   RACHAYA

LEBANON   DAMASCUS

Zahrani

SYRIA

NABATIYA   MARJAYOUN

Litani

TYRE

KIRYAT SHEMONA   UNDOF
Golan Heights

NAKOURA   QUNEITRA

Sept 1982 – Feb/April 1984
US, French, Italian and British military presence in West Beirut

●●●●● BEIRUT'S 'GREEN LINE'
ISRAELI FRONT LINES:
——— UP TO 2 SEPT 1983
●●●●● 4 SEPT 1983

0 MILES 20
0 KILOMETERS 30

©Richard Natkiel, 1984   To Haifa   ISRAEL

PLO the medieval crusaders' stronghold of Beaufort Castle, which was subsequently taken over by Haddad, and then proceeded to Nabatiyeh. The third force moved from the Golan Heights and on its way dealt with the PLO's militant wing, El Fatah, which was present in strength on the slopes of Mount Hermon. To this massive advance on three fronts the UNIFIL forces offered what was described as 'nonviolent opposition,' thereby demonstrating once again that peace-keeping forces can only keep the peace so long as both the hostile parties actually want peace.

Syrian forces, in Lebanon as the Arab Deterrent Force, presented a possible threat to the Israeli advance but were soon neutralized by a crushing Israeli air victory. On 8/9 June, according to Israeli figures, 60 Syrian aircraft were shot down for the loss of a single Israeli machine, thereby giving Israel superiority in the air over its troops in Lebanon. The pre-

LEFT: *Druze soldiers of the IDF mount guard in the Bekaa Valley in November 1982.*
RIGHT and BELOW: *Israeli artillerymen load and fire Katyusha rockets during fighting in the Beirut area in August 1982.*

ABOVE: *Residents of West Beirut rush to obtain water during a lull in the shelling by the besieging Israeli forces.*
FAR RIGHT: *Troops of the Multinational Force in the Sinai parade during 1982.*

ABOVE: *Lebanese youths rollerskate by parked Israeli tanks on the outskirts of Beirut in August 1982.*
FAR RIGHT: *Suspected PLO terrorists are led off blindfolded for interrogation.*

requisite of this victory was the destruction of the Syrian SAM-6 missile sites, achieved by the dispatch of pilotless Israeli reconnaissance aircraft ('drones') to the sites, which promptly shot them down but, in doing so, disclosed the locations and the radio frequencies of the missile sites. That was all the information needed for the

Israelis to contrive sufficient electronic countermeasures to enable ground-attack aircraft to hit the sites with little risk.

From mid-June the Israelis were besieging and bombarding Beirut, where the main forces and leadership of the PLO were located. High casualties were inflicted on the citizens, and a ceasefire

agreement was reached in August. The PLO forces, as well as Syrian troops, left the city, the PLO men being sent to other Arab states. Israel lifted the siege, and an international peacekeeping force was installed. Yasser Arafat, the PLO leader, went first to Greece to symbolize his disappointment with the Arab states, which

had hardly lifted a finger on behalf of the PLO during these events. In the following year Arafat was back in Lebanon, this time in the north, at Tripoli. Here he was assailed by former members of his organization, who had broken away in protest at what they considered to be his soft line. That soft line, nevertheless, had included a rejection of proposed peace settlements that would have permitted the continued existence of Israel while giving the Palestinians their own state.

In 1983 it became evident that the Israeli incursion into Lebanon had not brought the expected gains, and was of doubtful morality. Even in 1982 various members of the IDF had protested at what they had been ordered to do in Lebanon. This feeling of guilt and failure was intensified after Phalangists had massacred the inhabitants of two Palestinian refugee camps on the outskirts of Beirut. Israeli forces had been nearby at the time of these atrocities, but had not acted to prevent

BELOW: *An IDF Air Force Sikorsky S-65 helicopter ferries supplies into a camp south of the Beirut-Damascus Road.*

BOTTOM RIGHT: *An Israeli M109 self-propelled gun in action during the summer of 1982.*

them. The ensuing scandal, apart from compelling Sharon to resign, had the effect of polarizing Israeli public opinion, and the subsequent disputes between those who believed in military action and those who did not were of a bitterness not hitherto seen in Israel. Meanwhile, with Syria unwilling to withdraw its troops from Lebanon, Israel refused to withdraw its own forces from the south of that country, where they were subject to frequent guerrilla attacks. In this situation a way forward for Israel seemed hard to find, and it was a feeling of hopeless indecision that seems to have persuaded Begin to resign the premiership. By the end of February 1984, most of the international peacekeeping force had withdrawn, after the failure of the Lebanese Army in the face of attacks from Druze and Shia militia.

Other evidence of a more aggressive Israeli attitude had come in 1981. At the end of that year a series of measures was introduced which had the effect of annexing the Golan Heights; Israeli settlement was expected to follow as part of Begin's policy of 'creating facts' to transform his concept of an extended Israel from vision to reality. Earlier, there had been a far more dramatic event, when the Iraqi nuclear reactor at Tuwaitha was destroyed. For this operation, nine F16 ground-attack aircraft, escorted by five F15 fighters, flew into Iraq at a great height and by an indirect route, then dropped to low level to escape radar detection. This air attack without warning on a neighboring state aroused international condemnation, and the USA felt constrained to delay for some weeks further deliveries of F16 aircraft. Begin claimed that the raid was necessary because Iraq was developing the capacity to make a nuclear weapon, but his critics inside Israel claimed that the attack was timed so as to boost the Prime Minister's popularity on the eve of a general election.

ABOVE: *An Iranian soldier weeps by the body of his brother during an offensive on Abadan, 1980.*
TOP RIGHT: *As Syrian troops pulled out of Tripoli in Lebanon in July 1983, gunmen from the 24 October organization fired on them.*
RIGHT: *Iranian troops pose with a captured Iraqi M-60 tank during fighting on the outskirts of Abadan in October 1980.*

Iraq at the time had been engaged in a different war, which itself altered the balance of power in the Middle East. The disorganization that overtook Iran after the ousting of the Shah, and the ideological threat presented by Iran's new leader, Khomeini, tempted the Iraqi President Saddam Husain to start a war against Iran. He was supported by neighboring Arab states, who gave him financial help. At first, as Saddam Husain had expected, the Iraqis made great advances against a

surprised and already demoralized Iranian army. The Iraqi attack began in September 1980, and by the end of October Khorramshahr had been captured, as well as a belt of territory along the frontier. But a foreign attack was just what the Iranian regime needed to restore public order, invigorate the armed forces, and rally patriotic support around the government. In the beginning of 1981 the Iranians began to counterattack and during the next 18 months the Iraqis gradually lost the territory they had gained. Iraq's weapons were mainly of Russian provenance, and spares and supplies continued to come from the USSR. The Iranian forces had been built up by the USA during the Shah's regime and Iran, too, managed to obtain a large proportion of its needs during the war. However, both contestants took care to exclude the two superpowers from this theater. In the Persian Gulf area, where both Iran and Iraq had oil installations, the Iranians soon won naval and air superiority, although in late 1983 Iraq obtained five French Super Etendard aircraft with Exocet missiles, and with these began to attack shipping in the Gulf. Possibly Saddam Husain hoped that these formidable aircraft would persuade Khomeini to agree to a settlement, for Iraq by that

RIGHT: *Begin confers with Habib.*
CENTER RIGHT: *Small arms captured by Israeli forces piled up in Sidon, 1982.*
FAR RIGHT: *A Christian militiaman and IDF soldier man a checkpoint in Beirut.*
BELOW: *An IDF artilleryman relaxes by his M109 self-propelled gun.*

ABOVE: *Israel's Defense Minister Ariel Sharon Faces the Kahan Commission set up to investigate IDF complicity in the Lebanon massacres.*
OPPOSITE: *Palestinian women grieve for relatives massacred by Christian militiamen at the Sabra refugee camp in Lebanon.*

time was plainly suffering, and any hope of a short victorious war that would dispel the Baghdad regime's growing unpopularity had long since faded. Neither side reported convincing casualty figures, but it is evident that soldiers of both sides not only willingly faced death, but sought it. By the end of 1983 possibly about 50,000 Iraqis had been killed. Sacrificial counterattacks by the Iranians, often attempted by half-trained teenagers in a state of religious euphoria, meant that Iranian casualties were considerably greater than Iraqi, with deaths amounting to perhaps 200,000. These figures emphasize that this was the biggest of all modern Middle Eastern wars.

With a population of something like 14,000,000 against Iran's 41,000,000, Iraq would have seemed to have bitten off considerably more than it could chew. But population size in the Middle East gives little indication of immediate military potential. Iraq started the war with a

preponderance in most arms having, for example, about 2000 Soviet-built tanks to oppose the 800 Chieftains and 850 US-built tanks of Iran. The most startling relationship between population and armed strength was to be found in Israel which, with a population of 4,000,000, managed to field the most powerful army in the Middle East. In 1983 Israel had about 3600 main battle tanks, including some 250 home-designed and home-built *Merkavas* (the rest were Centurions, M48s, M60s, and ex-Soviet). It had about 550 combat aircraft, some of which were armed with Sidewinder missiles, and those aircraft included 150 home-built Kfir machines (Skyhawk, F4, F15 and F16 aircraft accounted for most of the rest). Its navy, though small, used the home-built Gabriel missile, which was superior to the missiles of Soviet-built ships in the Syrian Navy. Other missile strength lay in Hawk antiaircraft installations and Lance medium-range surface-to-surface launchers. With total mobilization, the IDF could muster 500,000 men and women.

Of Israel's enemies, Jordan and Libya had smaller populations, but Libya, with about 2800 Soviet-built tanks, 500 combat aircraft (mainly MiG-21, -23, and -25, but including some Mirages), and 70 *Scud* medium-range surface-to-surface mis-

siles, was on paper a formidable enemy. The distance separating Israel and Libya, while no obstacle to rhetoric, made it unlikely that Libya's full strength would be used against Israel. Jordan, which was no longer an inevitable enemy, had less than 100 aircraft and about 500 tanks.

Syria, with a population of 9,000,000 and ample supplies of Soviet weapons, was obviously Israel's main enemy, especially as the Golan Heights annexation was regarded in Damascus as temporary and to be reversed as soon as possible. In 1983 Syria had about 223,000 men under arms, of whom about 40,000 were in Lebanon. About 4000 Soviet-built tanks were on the inventory, including almost 1000 of the modern T72 type and over 1000 T62 units. The Syrian Navy had 18 missile boats while the Air Force was almost as large as Israel's, with roughly 450 combat aircraft. Some 200 of the latter were MiG-21s, about 100 were MiG-23s, and the rest were MiG-17s, SU-7s and SU-20s. Soviet *Scud* missiles, capable of hitting Israeli cities, were also in service.

Israel's northern neighbor, Lebanon, was hardly in a position to wage a serious war in 1983, although parts of its army remained loyal to the government. However, that army had been small in any case, with barely 60 tanks, supported by an air force consisting of one Hunter squadron.

ALL PICTURES: *The harrowing scenes following the two-day massacre of Palestinians in the Sabra refugee camp in West Beirut, September 1982.*

In the Middle East power is not reckoned by military strength alone. The oil-rich Gulf states had made small contributions of men in several Arab-Israeli conflicts, but their main significance was as providers of money. Saudi Arabian money, for example, backed Egypt in the period leading to the Yom Kippur War, and backed Iraq in its expensive war against Iran. Saudi Arabia was not negligible as an armed power, with its 300 AMX and 150 M60 tanks and its 175 combat aircraft (mainly F5 and F15 machines, but including a handful of British-built Lightnings). In late 1981 the USA permitted the export to Saudi Arabia of electronic surveillance and control aircraft (AWACs). This immediately enhanced Saudi Arabia's strategic situation, for these aircraft, among other things, could watch the activity of the Israeli Air Force and might, claimed the Israelis, give vital information to Israel's enemies in time of war. That the

USA ignored Israel's protests and gave Saudi Arabia what it demanded illustrated the changing balance in the Middle East, with the USA reverting to a policy of cultivating selected Arab states.

Nowhere was this new policy more evident than in Egypt where, despite the murder of Sadat, a continuing intimacy between Cairo and Washington developed after 1973. With its population of 46,000,000 and armed forces of nearly 500,000, Egypt was the dominant Arab power in the region. The process of changing back to Western weapons was a source of weakness perhaps, but Egypt was militarily stronger than she had ever been, and yet seemed to have no clearly defined likely enemy. For Egypt this was an agreeable situation that should have enabled resources to be devoted to internal economic and social development, and to some extent this did happen, but the forces of conservatism continued to hinder the

government in this endeavor.

The weakening of the PLO, which for the most part had kept the interests of the Palestinian refugees as its first priority, promised to change the Middle Eastern situation. Both the moderates, favoring a final compromise settlement, and the extremists who held fast to the aim of destroying Israel as a state, seemed likely to draw strength from the PLO's difficulties. If the moderates were to prevail, the settlement would doubtless bear, with one exception, a likeness to the 1937 proposal for a Jewish state and an Arab state in Palestine, with a special status for Jerusalem. The exception was that the Jewish state, as a consequence of a half-century of argument and conflict, would be considerably larger than that envisaged by the British 1937 Royal Commission. Inhabitants of the Middle East, who directly or indirectly had suffered conflict for decade after decade, would be entitled

to ask whether it had all been worthwhile. It was this same likelihood, of awkward questions being asked, that was one of the main reasons why Arab leaders were so reluctant to accept a settlement; and so long as they refused to compromise, the Israelis were spared the difficult obligation of deciding, or revealing, exactly what they wanted.

RIGHT: *An F-4 Phantom flying from a carrier of the US Sixth Fleet in the Mediterranean intercepts a pair of Tupolev Tu-22 Blinder medium bombers of the Libyan Air Force.*
BELOW RIGHT: *Moshe Arens greets Jeanne Kirkpatrick in March 1983.*
BOTTOM RIGHT: *Shultz talks to Begin during his shuttle diplomacy in 1983.*
BELOW: *United States Marines come ashore at Beirut to form part of the Multinational Peacekeeping Force in the city, August 1982.*

BELOW: *The USSR has supplied its MiG-23 Flogger fighter to several Middle East air arms, including those of Syria and Libya. A Libyan MiG-23 is pictured.*
INSET: *Israel's US-supplied F-16 Fighting Falcons have consistently outfought the Syrian Air Force in the Bekaa Valley, Lebanon.*

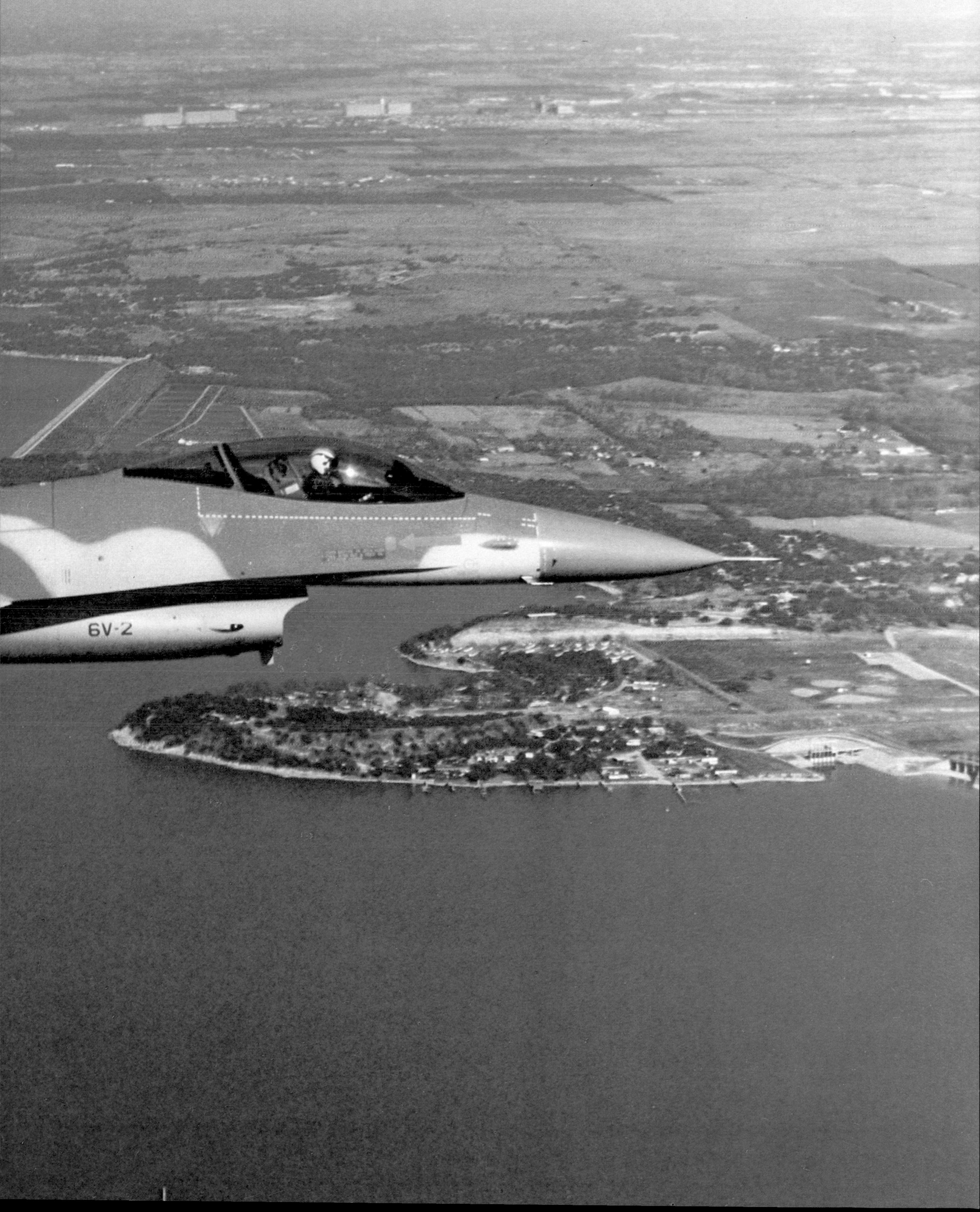
6V-2

A Chronology of the
PALESTINE LIBERATION ORGANIZATION

January 1964
PLO established at the first Arab 'summit' conference in Cairo. Its purpose is to co-ordinate the activities of the score or so guerrilla organizations. Of these, the following soon emerge as dominant: Al Fatah, led by Yasser Arafat; the Marxist Popular Front for the Liberation of Palestine (PFLP), led by George Habash; the Maoist Democratic Popular Front (DPF), led by Nayeb Hawatmeh; and Al Saiqa, sponsored by the Syrian Baath Party. These soon spawn breakaway groups. At the same time the Palestine Liberation Army (PLA) is founded.

October 1965
Leader of PLO, Ahmed Shukeiri, complains of scant support offered by Arab states.

June 1966
Shukeiri rejects allegations that PLO is communist-inclined, and defends right to acquire arms from China.

October 1966
Al Fatah wing of PLO intensifies guerrilla attacks on Israel border areas.

November 1966
In radio broadcasts from Cairo, Shukeiri describes King Hussein of Jordan as an atheistic murderer, tool of imperialism, and enemy of Islam and the Arabs.

May 1967
Shukeiri calls on Jordanians to overthrow Hussein.

March 1968
Syrian government arrests PFLP leaders to prevent raids from Syrian territory into Israel, but encourages Al Fatah to make raids from Jordan.

December 1968
PFLP attacks Israeli airliner at Athens. Israelis raid Beirut in retaliation, virtually destroying Lebanon's airline (MEA) with consequent heavy loss (about £8,000,000) for the insurers, Lloyds of London.

February 1969
PFLP attacks Israeli airliner at Zurich.

August 1969
PFLP hijacks US airliner to Syria. PFLP makes bomb attacks against Israeli offices in foreign capitals. Such raids, and hijacks, are repeated in subsequent months.

June 1970
Heavy fighting in Amman between guerrillas and Jordanian Army. Arafat, now head of PLO while retaining leadership of Al Fatah, signs agreement on ceasefire with King Hussein.

September 1970
PFLP hijacks four airliners, including US and British. Hijack of Israeli aircraft over Britain fails. Arrival of hijacked aircraft in Jordan causes renewed tension between government and guerrillas. Jordanian Army begins successful campaign to eliminate guerrilla movement on Jordanian territory.

November 1971
Black September group, dedicated to the destruction of King Hussein and of Israel, assassinates Jordanian premier.

May 1972
Israelis successfully storm Belgian airliner hijacked at Lod Airport. Later, Japanese terrorists acting for PFLP kill many passengers at Lod Airport before being captured.

LEFT: *The son of a PLO guerrilla gives the victory sign as his father leaves West Beirut for Tunisia in August 1982.*
TOP RIGHT: *George Habash, leader of the Popular Front for the Liberation of Palestine.*
TOP FAR RIGHT: *Palestine guerrilla forces in Lebanon prepare to repel an Israeli reprisal raid on their camp.*
RIGHT: *Israeli troops examine a pile of arms captured from Palestinian guerrillas during the occupation of Sidon in 1982.*

July 1972
Bomb attacks on guerrilla leaders at Beirut; Israeli participation confirmed.

September 1972
Black September kills Israeli athletes at Munich Olympic Games. Letterbomb attempts at killing Israeli diplomats.

October 1972
Hijack of German airliner leads to release of terrorists arrested after Munich attack.

March 1973
Black September invades Saudi Arabian embassy in Khartoum, killing US and Belgian diplomats.

September 1973
Austria agrees to close transit camp for Jewish emigrants from USSR, after hijack of Austrian train. Failure of attempt to shoot down Israeli airliner at Rome with ground-to-air missiles.

May 1974
Continuing raids across Israeli frontier involve deaths of children at a school in Maalot.

June 1974
Fighting between rival guerrilla organizations in Beirut.

October 1974
Arab summit conference at Rabat recognizes PLO as sole representative of Palestinian people. UN General Assembly against Israeli and US opposition invites PLO to participate in debate about Palestine. Arafat addresses General Assembly.

October 1975
Unsuccessful armed attack, designed to release convicted hijackers from Dutch prison.

November 1975
Dissident Al Fatah group hijacks British aircraft but is condemned by PLO, anxious to preserve its recently won international respectability.

December 1975
Arm of the Arab Revolution group hijacks representatives of OPEC oil organization at Vienna, and is condemned both by PLO and PFLP.

June 1976
Israelis recapture French airliner hijacked to Entebbe. PFLP denies involvement and PLO condemns the hijacking. In Lebanon, Al Fatah continues the fight, begun in May, against Syrian troops and Lebanese Christians. Arafat maintains his hostility to Syrian presence in Lebanon.

March 1977
In Palestine National Council (PNC, the PLO's 'parliament') the strength of the moderates is increased at the expense of the rejectionists (those groups seeking not negotiations, but the destruction of Israel).

July 1978
Various PLO moderates assassinated in several countries.

May 1979
Continuing attacks on and by Palestinians abroad. Palestinian convicted for murder of Iraqi ambassador to Britain.

July 1979
Chancellor Kreisky of Austria becomes first head of government to meet formally with Arafat. Israel describes meeting as hostile act.

July 1980
Arafat calls on PLO to resist imminent Israeli attempt to destroy it in Lebanon.

July 1981
Heavy Israeli air attacks on PLO in Lebanon. PLO replies with rocket attacks on Israeli settlements.

April 1982
PLO denies responsibility for murder of Israeli diplomat in Paris. Israel chooses to reject this disclaimer.

May 1982
Renewal of Israeli air attacks on PLO in Lebanon. PLO resumes rocket attacks against Israel.

June 1982
Israel invades Lebanon to destroy PLO. Siege of Beirut begins.

August 1982
Siege of Beirut ends. Arafat and PLO in Beirut are removed from Lebanon.

September 1982
The Pope receives Arafat.

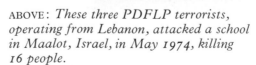

PREVIOUS PAGES: *Palestinian Liberation Organization troops await evacuation from Beirut.*
PREVIOUS PAGES, INSET: *PLO leader Yasser Arafat greets General Erskine, a Ghanaian member of the United Nations peacekeeping forces.*

ABOVE: *These three PDFLP terrorists, operating from Lebanon, attacked a school in Maalot, Israel, in May 1974, killing 16 people.*
RIGHT: *Lebanese Army troops and French Legionnaires stand by as PLO forces are evacuated from Beirut docks, August 1982.*

October 1982
Arafat and King Hussein begin discussions on US President Reagan's peace plan, which envisages a Palestine-Jordan federation.

January 1983
Several constituent groups of the PLO (including the PFLP but not Al Fatah) reject any settlement involving the establishment of a Zionist state. PLO representatives have quiet meetings with representatives of Israeli opposition parties.

February 1983
Conflict between moderates and rejectionists in PNC. Dr Sartawi, chief PLO adviser, resigns after being prevented by Arafat from speaking in favor of recognition of Israel. PNC denounces use of terrorism.

April 1983
Dr Sartawi murdered in Portugal by breakaway group, the Revolutionary Council of Al Fatah. Arafat-Hussein talks break down.

May 1983
Al Fatah leaders, led by Abu Musa, condemn Arafat for appointing his favorites and for negotiating with Hussein. Arafat accuses Syria and Libya of supporting Abu Musa faction. Fighting breaks out as Arafat forcibly attempts to end this revolt. Other groups in PLO take sides.

June 1983
Syria expels Arafat, who moves with his supporters to Tripoli. With an occasional helping hand from Israel, and a frequent helping hand from Syria, the anti-Arafat groups gain strength.

December 1983
Despite ceasefires in July and August, factional hostilities continue and Arafat and his supporters are forced to evacuate Tripoli by means of ships provided by the Greek government.

A member of the Palestinian Liberation Organization, swathed in the characteristic checked scarf, awaits evacuation from Beirut.

INDEX

ACKNOWLEDGMENTS

The publisher would like to thank Design 23 for designing this book, Stephanie Lindsay and John Crowley for picture research, David Hawthorne for preparing the index, Jane Laslett, the editor, and the individuals and agencies below for supplying the photographs: AP World Wide pp 4-5, 13, 17 (top), 18 (below) 22-23, 24, 30-31, 59, 60 (below), 64 (below), 66 (bottom), 68, 94 (top), 99 (below), 101, 104-105 (main pic), 110-111, 112, 114-115 (below), 118 (both), 119, 128, 129 (both), 141 (below), 148, 150-151, 152 (top), 163 (main pic), 162 (right), 163 (main pic), 167 (main pic), 173 (top), 176 (top), 178-179 (all pix), 184, 188; Camera Press pp 186-87 (main pic), 190; General Dynamics pp 182-183 (main pic); IDF Archives pp 8, 16 (top), 17 (below), 16 (top), 21 (right), 25 (both); IDF courtesy/Bahamane pp 55, 61 (top); Imperial War Museum pp 9 (above), 10, 56 (center and bottom), 57 (center and bottom), 65 (both); Israeli Government Press Office pp 1, 12 (top and bottom), 16 (below), 18 (top), 19 (both), 20 (both), 21 (top and left), 26 (both), 27 (both), 29 (both), 32, 34 (below), 35 (both), 36-37, 38-39, 40, 41, 42, 43 (both), 44, 45 (both), 46-47 (both), 48-49 (both), 50-51 (both), 52 (all three), 53 (both), 60 (top), 64 (top), 72 (top), 74-75 (main pic), 76 (both), 77 (both), 78, 80-81, 82, 83 (both), 84, 85, 86, 88, 89, 90-91, 92-93, 94 (bottom two), 95, 96 (all 3), 97, 98, 99 (top), 100, 102-103 (both), 105 (inset), 106-107, 108-109, 113, 114 (top), 115 (top), 116 (both), 117, 120-121 (both), 124, 125, 132 (all 3), 133 (both), 134 (both), 136 (both), 137, 138, 140 (both), 141 (top), 142-43 (main pic), 144-145, 152 (center and bottom), 153 (all 3), 155 (both), 156-157 (both), 158 (inset), 160 (both), 161 (top), 162 (left), 164-165 (all 3), 168-169 (both), 170-171 (both), 174-175 (all pix), 176 (below), 177, 180, 181 (center and bottom), 185 (top left and bottom), 189; Keystone Press Agency pp 9 (below), 33 (both), 34 (top), 56 (top), 57 (top), 58, 62-63, 66 (top), 67, 69 (both), 70 (both), 71, 73 (below), 79, 122-123, 126, 127, 172, 173 (below), 185 (top right); Richard Natkiel (maps) pp 14, 54, 87, 95, 100, 135, 139, 142, 146, 159, 162; Robert Hunt Library pp 72 (below), 73 (top), 74 (inset), 143 (inset); Robert Young L11P pp back jacket, 2-3, 6-7, 11, 12 (center), 14, 15, 28 (both); Syrian Government Press Office pp 139, 161 (below); UN/Y Nagata pp 147, 149; UN pp 158-159 (main pix), 187 (inset), 130-131, 187 (inset); USAF pp 154 (below), 163 (inset), 182 (inset); US Army pp 154 (top), 167 (inset); US Marine Corps pp 66 (center); US Navy p 181 (top).